Information Systems Engineering Library
SSADM Version 4 Preliminary Guide

SSADM and GUI Design: a Project Manager's Guide

LONDON: HMSO

April 1994

SSADM and GUI Design: a Project Manager's Guide

This Preliminary Guide has been produced by the GUI Working Group with the approval of the ISUG Technical Committee. As a working document, it provides a useful example of how SSADM can be customised to take advantage of particular technologies, and as such is welcomed by the SSADM Design Authority Board.

Rob Herson (LBMS) Chairman
Graham Berrisford (Model Systems)
Tony Betts (CCTA)
Dermot Browne (KPMG Management Consulting)
Ian Clowes (Logica)
Eric Davie (CCTA)
Peter Gough
Arthur Haynes
David Redmond-Pyle (LBMS)
Jennifer Stapleton (Logica)
Alfie Windsor (Interskill Consulting)

© International SSADM Users Group Ltd 1994

Applications for reproduction should be made to HMSO

First Published 1994

ISBN 0 11 330650 4

Table of Contents

1 Introduction   7

    1.1   Purpose of this Preliminary Guide   7

    1.2   Who should read this guide?   7

    1.3   Status of this guide   8

    1.4   Authors   8

2 Overview   9

    2.1   Graphical User Interface Technology   9

    2.2   GUI Misconceptions   10

    2.3   User Interface Development   11

    2.4   User-centred Design   14

    2.5   Style Guides   16

    2.6   User-centred versus System-centred Approaches   17

    2.7   Usability   18

    2.8   Business Benefits   19

    2.9   Contents of this guide   19

    2.10   Summary   20

3 Project Management   21

    3.1   Introduction   21

    3.2   Tailoring of the Method   22

    3.3   Changes of Approach   23

    3.4   Changes to the Team and Roles   23

    3.5   Implications for Project Management   25

4	**Techniques and Products**		**29**
	4.1	Introduction	29
	4.2	User Analysis	33
	4.3	Usability Analysis	37
	4.4	Task Modelling	41
	4.5	Task Scenario Definition	46
	4.6	Style Guide Definition	48
	4.7	User Conceptual Modelling	54
	4.8	GUI Design	62
	4.9	User Interface Prototyping	67
	4.10	GUI Evaluation	72
5	**Tailoring of the Default SSADM Structural Model**		**77**
	5.1	Introduction	77
	5.2	Stage 1	78
	5.3	Stage 2	81
	5.4	Stage 3	82
	5.5	Stage 4	88
	5.6	Stage 5	91
	5.7	Stage 6	92
6	**Tailored approaches to systems development using SSADM Version 4**		**95**
	6.1	Introduction	95
	6.2	The system development template and the 3-schema specification architecture	96

6.3	User-centered design and the system development template	99

Bibliography 103

Glossary of Terms 107

List of Figures

Figure 4-1: Product Flow Diagram 31

Figure 4-2: User Class Matrix 35

Figure 4-3: The Role of the Users' Conceptual Model 61

Figure 5-1: SSADM Structural Model - Stage 1 80

Figure 5-2: SSADM Structural Model - Stage 2 83

Figure 5-3: SSADM Structural Model - Stage 3 86

Figure 5-4: SSADM Structural Model - Stage 4 89

Figure 5-5: SSADM Structural Model - Stage 5 90

Figure 5-6: SSADM Structural Model - Stage 6 93

Figure 6-1: System Development Template 96

Figure 6-2: System Development Template and 3-schema architecture 97

Figure 6-3: Mapping of Product Flow Diagram onto system development template 100

SSADM and GUI Design: a Project Manager's Guide

For further information regarding this publication and other services please contact:

- International SSADM Users Group Limited,
  11 Burlings Lane,
  Knockholt,
  Kent   TN14 7PB

Telephone: 0959 534337

Facsimile: 0959 534184

1 Introduction

1.1 Purpose of this Preliminary Guide

This preliminary guide has been written for managers of SSADM projects which are going to employ Graphical User Interface (GUI) technology. The guide introduces the reader to the techniques necessary for the analysis, design, and testing of GUI Designs.

The use of SSADM for the delivery of GUI technology is a new area which is still evolving; and therefore, whilst this guide represents best practice, it cannot yet be considered definitive.

The major implications for project management of using GUI technology are the need for:

- increased involvement from end-users and user management;

- more emphasis on the usability aspects of user requirements analysis;

- specialist skills in Human-Computer Interaction techniques (HCI);

- appreciation of techniques beyond those presently in core SSADM.

This guide has been written to be compatible with core SSADM as published in the Version 4 Manual. A tailored Structural Model is included, which defines what needs to be done to build GUI systems using SSADM. Brief descriptions are provided for the additional products and techniques, supported by a product flow diagram which assists the connection with the original method.

1.2 Who should read this guide?

This guide is for managers of SSADM projects intending to employ GUI technology. Having said this, the techniques introduced are equally applicable to 4GL environments and character based user interfaces.

In addition, the guide will be of value to analysts, designers, user representatives, computer auditors, and quality assurance staff involved in projects utilising GUI technology.

1.3 Status of this guide	This Preliminary Guide has been developed by the GUI Working Group of the International SSADM Users Group (ISUG), and has been reviewed by the ISUG Technical Committee. The Technical Committee strongly recommend its use on SSADM projects employing a graphical user interface, since it is well founded on current HCI practice.

The HCI community has various techniques and notations for developing the products described in the Guide. Depending on the method used, each product can be represented in several different ways. Therefore, it has not been possible to include the examples which would be required in a detailed Practitioners' Guide.

As a Preliminary Guide on this topic, it has not been possible to resolve all the issues that arise in integrating HCI and SSADM techniques and approaches (eg the role of I/O Structures). Of particular concern is the proposed tailoring of the Structural Model, which makes the logical/physical divide less clear than the philosophy of SSADM would indicate.

Nevertheless, with these reservations, the Technical Committee is happy to endorse the contents of this Guide.

1.4 Authors — This guide has been developed by practitioners in SSADM Version 4 and/or user-centred design. It is intended to represent a sensible blending of these disciplines.

Commonly accepted Human Computer Interface (HCI) terminology has been used wherever appropriate. This will allow easier understanding of the literature referenced in this guide.

2 Overview

2.1 Graphical User Interface Technology

In order to explain what a Graphical User Interface (GUI) is, it is first necessary to explain what a user interface is.

A user interface is any aspect of a system that impacts a user's interaction with that system. When contemplating the phrase 'user interface', an image of a computer screen, possibly filled with windows and colours, often comes to mind. While this image is accurate, it is also incomplete. User interfaces must be considered as including all training materials, input devices, workplace furniture, the workplace environment, and other users.

GUIs are a sub-set of user interface considerations which deal with the technology for the on-screen aspects of user interaction with Information Technology (IT).

In principle, GUIs provide an effective technology to support communication between users and Information Technology. GUIs are characterised by a number of components, collectively referred to by the acronym WIMP (Windows, Icons, Menus, Pointers):

- **Windows:** equate broadly to virtual 'screens' except that users can have multiple windows open simultaneously on a single physical screen. Also, the size and position of individual windows is under user control.

- **Icons:** are on-screen images used to represent objects or actions of interest to users. For instance, an image of a wastebasket might be used to represent a repository for objects that the user wishes to delete.

- **Menus:** commands are represented as lists from which the user can select.

- **Pointers:** selection is most often supported by a Mouse as an alternative to keyboard entry. The mouse controls an on- screen pointer, which is used to 'point at and select' representations of buttons, icons, menu options, etc. Alternatively, objects might be selected and then 'dragged and dropped' onto other reserved screen areas. For instance, invoking the printing of a report might be achieved by selecting the report and then dragging and dropping its image onto a representation of a printer.

There are a number of GUI products on the market, but 'windows' is the collective term commonly used to refer to them.

While it might be thought that the usability of products will inevitably improve through the provision of Graphical User Interfaces and application of 'Look and Feel Guidelines', a paradox exists. The greater flexibility for design afforded by GUIs actually means that there is more opportunity for creating poor designs. Standards do not resolve this problem: they merely provide a framework and a set of constraints within which it is suggested any design should fit.

Well designed GUIs provide user interfaces which are quick to learn, productive, and satisfying for users. By understanding the target user population in terms of their capabilities and task requirements, good designs can be produced. Ideally, designs should make it easier for users to accomplish their tasks.

2.2 GUI Misconceptions

GUIs are not the same as client/server technology. It is true that client/server projects usually employ GUI technology, but this is not essential.

Using GUI technology does not pre-suppose the use of object oriented techniques. The use of GUIs encourages the modelling of objects as *things of interest* to users. As a result, projects may choose to take an object oriented approach to development. The adoption of such an approach to the development of GUIs is neither mandatory nor essential.

2.3 User Interface Development

Estimates suggest that on GUI developments, more than 50% of the code and 30% of development expenditure can be for the GUI alone. As the complexity of user interface components increases, and users become even more demanding, it can be expected that these figures will rise further.

In addition, analysis has shown that upwards of 60% of the total cost of a software system is incurred during the maintenance phase of the software life-cycle. Furthermore, it has been estimated that 60% of maintenance costs are for changes to the user interface.

Taking these figures for development and maintenance together suggests that improvements in user interface design practices could bring major productivity gains to the IT industry. The application of user-centred design techniques offers a means to realise these productivity gains.

2.3.1 Why is User Interface Design not Practised?

There has been a lack of uptake in the IT industry of the techniques underlying user interface design. There may be many reasons for this. Two possible reasons are proposed below:

- Resistance to new techniques.

Many people are resistant to proposals that seek to add new techniques to the system development process. This is an understandable yet untenable view. Existing methods, including core SSADM, were developed at a time when interfaces were delivered through dumb terminals. The advent of GUI technology has added a new dimension by providing a means to develop more usable systems at the cost of additional complexity. It is this additional complexity which creates the need for new techniques.

- Belief that the techniques are being practised.

There is no doubt that some of the techniques advocated by user interface designers are being practised. Unfortunately, they are infrequently practised in the way intended. Prototyping is a prime example. Prototypes are often developed and used to guide design, even though they are never tested with actual or prospective users. In addition, the techniques that are available exist like islands, with no bridges between one and the next. This guide discusses the relationships between the various techniques, and places them within the framework of SSADM.

2.3.2 Why is User Interface Design important?

The growing population of computer users are becoming more demanding. Users now want the data access capabilities offered presently through dumb terminals to be integrated with the usability offered by PCs.

International bodies are now championing the call for usable systems. The Department of Trade and Industry in the United Kingdom ran a campaign entitled *Usability Now*, with the twin objectives of raising awareness of the benefits to be gained from well designed user interfaces, and educating industry as to where advice can be found. A European Commission Directive (90/270/EC) on the "minimum safety and health requirements for work with display screen equipment" demands a response from each European member state. These responses must include procedures for establishing working practices that include assessment of how well systems support their users.

In response to this directive, the Health and Safety Executive in the United Kingdom has published a document entitled "Display Screen Equipment Work: Guidance on Regulations". The British Standards Institute is also producing a set of standards (BSI 92/35512 DC) with respect to the provision of usable systems. In Europe, the ISO (International Organisation for Standardisation) body and the CEN (Comit Europeen de Normalisation) are producing standards covering similar issues. Standards and legislation will be forced upon IT procurers, and they in turn will expect suppliers to provide systems that meet the standards. These standards will certainly raise awareness within the business community of the need to design for users. This awareness will lead to an increased demand for skilled user interface designers and supporting techniques.

2.3.3 What is a system?

IT alone does not make a system. Not until technology is placed in the hands of users, and is employed in anger, can it truly be called a system. While data analyses, functional analyses, business analyses, and process analyses are all necessary to varying degrees on different projects, the designs that result are all failing if that essential system component, the user, is not taken into account adequately.

It has been commonplace for the industry to generate accurate and complete functional specifications that procurers endorse without full understanding. Subsequently, a fully functional and accurate system, according to the specification, is delivered only to be met with the response "that is not how we thought it would be". The poor communication of requirements may explain such a scenario.

This problem is well known. One response to it has been an increasing interest in prototyping activities, with the intention of giving end-users an early and realistic sight of the analysts' understanding of what is required. Unfortunately, prototypes are not the complete answer. All too often, prototypes are not seen by actual users but rather by user representatives who are not very representative. Prototyping is often planned in such a manner that the prototype itself becomes a fait accompli. Prototypes may not be tested in a sufficiently rigorous manner to ensure that design inadequacies are trapped.

Users viewing a prototype may genuinely agree that it is a vast improvement over what went before; but because they are not IT specialists, they may fail to identify or convey how the design could be improved. It is for these reasons that user interface provision must be regarded as an iterative design activity. Adequate user requirements must be afforded to designers who can then apply their experience, and best practice, to produce designs well suited to their purpose. Such designers need to be aware of what is possible with the technology at hand, what the limitations and abilities of the user population are, and the use to which the technology will be put. Thus user interface designers are a specialist band, knowledgable about user interfacing technology, trained in task analysis, and educated in human behaviour.

No longer is the IT industry preoccupied with making IT work. The problem now is getting IT to work effectively with users. To support the growing population of increasingly demanding users, appreciably more resources are being directed towards providing quality user interfaces. There is international recognition that this shift in effort needs to be supported by better practices.

2.4   User-centred Design

User-centred design is a set of techniques for the development of user interfaces displaying high quality usability. When applied properly, user-centred design ensures the ultimate usability of interactive systems.

The techniques included in user-centred design are: User Analysis; Usability Analysis; Task Modelling; Task Scenario Definition; Style Guide Definition; User Conceptual Modelling; GUI Design; User Interface Prototyping; and GUI Evaluation.

User Analysis provides a detailed understanding of end-users to help guide the user interface design process.

While Usability Analysis bears many similarities to Systems Analysis, it has the specific aim of collecting data pertaining to the design of user interfaces, as distinct from purely functional or computational components of a system.

Task Modelling takes the results of Usability Analysis, and produces Task Models using one of a number of notations or descriptions to capture the dependencies, sequencing, selection, parallelism, etc., that exist in task execution.

Task Scenario Definition documents represent instances of task execution for use during the design process, particularly evaluation.

Chapter 2
Overview

Style Guide Definition determines a set of rules that the user interface design must obey. The intention is to produce consistent interfaces that permit users to generalise their skills between and within applications.

User Conceptual Modelling builds on the results of Task Modelling to produce a model for the system that will be of value to users. That is, User Conceptual Modelling sets out specifically to provide a model independently of any data models that the system may have to encompass. User Conceptual Models provide a model of the system's data and operation that users will be able to assimilate easily and work with effectively. User Conceptual Modelling relies heavily on the skills of user interface designers.

GUI Design takes the results of Task Modelling and User Conceptual Modelling, and within the constraints of the Style Guide delivers a User Interface Design.

User Interface Prototyping is performed to provide an interactive view of the intended design. While prototypes may not be provided for the whole of the system's user interface, they are intended to be realistic and be critiqued by users. Importantly, they must be sufficiently robust to allow evaluation by end-users, not simply demonstrated to end-users. Given that prototype evaluation is a skilled undertaking, it is recommended that assistance is sought from an HCI practitioner.

GUI Evaluations assess the usability and suitability of a user interface design as exemplified by a User Interface Prototype.

User-centred design techniques need to be selected to meet the needs of particular projects. For instance, when a Style Guide already exists, a new one may not be needed. Similarly, when applied in conjunction with core SSADM, there will be a need for the appropriate SSADM and user-centred design techniques to be selected, to avoid duplication of effort. In addition, the sequence in which the various techniques are applied should be managed carefully. The integration of core SSADM and user-centred design techniques is discussed in more detail in Chapter 5.

This guide suggests that most techniques are practised during Stage 3 of SSADM, including GUI Design and Evaluation. SSADM pracitioners may think it unusual to include design activities during the Requirements Specification Module. The reason for this is that practice has shown that User Interface Prototyping, particularly prototype evaluation, is an excellent technique for analysing requirements, and as such should take place at a time in the life-cycle at which it can contribute to Requirements Specification.

2.5 Style Guides

One of the most talked about topics in the computer industry is the issue of Style Guides, or 'Look and Feel Guidelines' to be employed for user interfaces. A number of these now exist, including ***CUA*** (IBM 1991), the ***Apple Human Interface Guidelines*** (1993a and b), ***OSF/MOTIF*** from the Open Software Foundation (1993), ***The Windows Interface, an Application Design Guide*** from Microsoft (1992), and ***Open Look*** from AT&T and Sun (1989).

The advantages of such guidelines are that they determine a certain style and consistency for user interaction. For instance, all commands might be chosen from pull-down menus, the close window function is always performed by clicking on a certain part of the window's frame, etc. Such guidelines can offer benefits, particularly where users are expected to move between and use different applications in the course of their job. A knowledge of the in-house style can be transferred to many different applications without necessitating extensive re-training.

Where a set of guidelines is adopted, it is still necessary to perform analyses to support interface design. For instance, no style guideline can dictate appropriate literals (ie command names), determine the appropriate positioning of windows, or in fact their content. Dialogue sequencing, format of information, content of warnings, error messages, help texts, etc, also have to be determined as a design exercise.

- Style guidelines do not provide design solutions. They only constrain the design space in order that consistency can be achieved. Whilst consistency is a good design principle, it alone cannot guarantee usability.

GUIs and interface standards are not a panacea for usability. GUIs offer greater scope for design, and consequently more opportunity for poor design. Adopting guidelines helps to identify the design issues. Resolution of these issues can then be achieved through careful consideration of end-user requirements, and how they can best be supported.

- The assumption that the adoption of GUI technology will ensure usability is a fallacy.

2.6 User-centred versus System-centred Approaches

System developers tend to create engineering models based on data and/or functions. For instance, in the past, database management systems required users to be aware of the data structures being used for data storage. Thus, users of relational databases had to perform operations such as the joining of tables. Users found this extremely cumbersome, difficult to understand, and an overhead they would happily forego. The most appropriate model for user interface design must be based on the needs of end-users, in terms of what they wish to accomplish with the system. User-centred design achieves this by determining a suitable conceptual model with which users can work.

User interface design should begin with an understanding of the tasks the system is going to support. That is, what are the requirements of the end-users of that system? What are the capabilities of those users? Which functions should remain under user control, and which under system control? In what sequence are tasks to be completed? What information does the user require in order to progress each task? What method of interaction will best support these tasks?

These are just a few of the questions to which a user requirements analysis provides answers, in order to establish a task model from which user interface design can progress. By performing task modelling early in a development, an outline user interface design can be produced. By so doing, requirements will be identified that will need to be addressed by the engineering model of a system as essential functionality.

This guide recommends a user-centred design approach to GUI design, in which the primary influences on the GUI are the end-users, their usability requirements, tasks, and capabilities. Alternative approaches do exist, including the system-centred approach to GUI design (Robinson and Berrisford 1994) in which entities, events and enquiries are defined first, and used to design (or even generate) the initial GUI.

A system-centred approach has the disadvantage of leading to an interface design which is not as usable as it should be. On the other hand, a system-centred approach has advantages. It gives more rapid application development. It encourages greater reuse of code. It ensures that all required functions (even obscure and infrequent functions the user does not realise will be needed) are supported by a basic user interface.

In practice a user-centred design must be integrated with the database update and enquiry processes, which means bringing user-centred and system-centred views into harmony.

2.7 Usability

Usability addresses how well users can make use of the functionality of a system. This is distinct from utility, which refers to whether the functionality of a system can do what is needed. A system can have potential utility while being less than useful operationally. Usability refers to an operational quality, whereas utility can be assessed non-operationally.

Usability criteria or usability metrics are quantifiable measures that can be taken for an interactive system. They are dependent on having a user interacting with that system. That is, they cannot be obtained from observation of the system developer's interaction with the system, nor by having the system simulate interaction. In essence, the end-user cannot be eliminated from the system during usability assessment.

Five categories of criteria are often used. These are Productivity, Learnability, User satisfaction, Memorability, and Errors; together referred to as the PLUME measures.

Different projects will place different emphasis on different usability categories, depending on the objectives and context of the system in question.

2.8 Business Benefits

Delivering systems that demonstrate high usability provides business benefits. Training budgets are reduced as users can practice generic computer literacy skills without learning many and varied command languages. Productivity increases ensue where a better match is achieved between end-user requirements and system support. Appropriately supported jobs can lead to a reduction in staff turnover, and a commensurate reduction in recruitment and training costs. Utilising GUI components such as pick lists and context sensitive dialogues facilitates reduced error rates, and a reduction in associated reconciliation costs. Jobs may be enriched, and flexibility of staffing may be achieved as users can transfer skills between applications designed to be consistent. Each of these factors has an associated financial benefit.

The design of the GUI is instrumental in determining the ultimate value of a system. Poor designs have a detrimental effect on usability, and in turn undermine the business benefits that might have been gained. On the other hand, a well designed GUI will bring the business benefits that follow from improved usability.

2.9 Contents of this guide

This Chapter has described the reasons why a user-centred approach to the design of GUIs is needed.

Chapter 3 addresses the implications of using GUIs for

the project manager and other senior managers. It provides guidelines for managing a GUI based project, particularly where PRINCE is used. It summarises the effect on project management, project staffing and roles, workload estimation, and Quality Assurance (QA).

Chapter 4 describes in more detail the techniques of user-centred design, and the products of applying those techniques.

Chapter 5 provides a tailored version of the Structural Model for SSADM Version 4, including suggested changes to existing steps and additional steps specific to the design of GUIs.

Chapter 6 describes how the guidance relates to the SSADM rationale.

The **Bibliography** is provided for those readers requiring more detail on user-centred design in general, and the techniques specifically described in this guide.

Finally, there is a comprehensive **Glossary** of terms defining the non-SSADM terminology used within this guide.

2.10 Summary

It is inevitable that user-centred approaches to the development of user interfaces for interactive systems will become common place. The IT industry cannot continue to develop systems where upwards of 50% of the system code is for user interfacing purposes, by employing ill-suited practices; a new approach is needed.

This guide describes a set of techniques, and suggests how they could be used in conjunction with SSADM Version 4. It is hoped that this text will raise awareness of both the importance of user interface design, and demonstrate that techniques are available to be applied for the development of more usable systems. Moreover, that they can be applied in a structured and manageable manner within the constraints of projects employing SSADM Version 4.

3 Project Management

3.1 Introduction

The current novelty of GUI systems, especially when they are used with SSADM, increases the problems of all those involved in the management of a project.

This chapter sets out to highlight those areas where managers need to understand that change has occurred. The guidance is intended to supplement current standards, not to replace them. In many cases, the advice given reflects good practice that pertains equally well to non-GUI applications.

Use of GUIs with SSADM V4 is still evolving, and the advice in this guide will inevitably need to change as knowledge and experience are gained. However, the guidance is intended to enable more accurate planning for the products, skills, and resources that will be required, thus enabling a more realistic view of likely timescales. It is important, though, that project managers keep themselves informed of current developments.

This guide recommends a user-centred design approach to GUI design, in which the primary influences on the GUI are the end-users, their usability requirements, their tasks, and their mental models. The resulting GUI maps onto the SSADM constructs used to specify the underlying system.

An alternative is to use a system-centred design approach, in which the entities, events, and enquiries are defined first, and a GUI is designed in a mechanical way to support the events and enquiries. This event-driven approach by-passes Function Definition and Dialogue Design, and generates a crude user interface.

Both user-centred and system-centred design approaches may be used on the same SSADM project. User-centred design enhances the external design techniques within SSADM: user roles; functions; and dialogues.
User-centred design should be used where usability is an important requirement. System-centred design may be used for parts of the system where speed of development

SSADM and GUI Design: a Project Manager's Guide

is more important than usability; for example, maintenance of tables of reference data. The resulting initial GUI Design should be prototyped with end-users, and revised as necessary. Care must also be taken that using two approaches on a project does not result in the development of inconsistent interfaces.

3.2 Tailoring of the Method

3.2.1 Structural Model

The use of GUIs has a significant impact on the default Version 4 Structural Model:

- there are a number of additional steps, particularly in Stage 3.

- quite a few existing steps are changed. Some activities have been moved from one Stage to another.

- most significantly, the order of steps within a Stage is altered.

- Stage 2 should include the choice of prototyping environment.

- the scope of Stages 5 and 6 are reduced.

Project managers need to consider the changes proposed, and to understand how they will alter the timing of project activity and the additional skill levels that will be required to support the tailored Model's steps.

3.2.2 Techniques

Several additional techniques are needed in order to undertake some of the new activities arising from the use of a GUI. Project managers must ensure that staff understand the purpose of each, and are adequately trained in their application in time for their effective use on the project. From a quality management point of view, managers must define the impact of the additional and revised techniques in terms of the products to be developed.

Chapter 3
Project Management

3.2.3 Products

Inevitably, there are additions and subtractions in the product set. The additional products will need to be produced, and adequate arrangements established for their quality assurance; conversely, some products are no longer required.

The Style Guides are products that assume much greater importance in the GUI environment. The Installation Style Guide and the Application Style Guide are fundamental to the success of GUI projects, as they define the 'look-and-feel' of the system. The guides must be complete, at least in draft form, before detailed GUI design can commence. Other than for small or stand alone projects, development time for the Style Guides will often be measured in effort-months rather than effort-weeks.

3.3 Changes of Approach

The new approach reinforces the implied iterative nature of SSADM, while retaining defined steps and products that allow project progress to be monitored. Managers of SSADM projects that may involve a GUI will need to appreciate the iterative approach, particularly the impact it has upon the completeness and quality assurance of products.

One aspect of change, which merits particular mention, is that it may be necessary to make technical decisions much earlier than would normally be the case; for example, the choice of the GUI environment and its hardware configuration.

3.4 Changes to the Team and Roles

3.4.1 User involvement

For a GUI-based system to be successful, the early stages of analysis and requirements definition rely more than ever on extensive user involvement. Understanding the users' needs and how they perceive those needs is therefore fundamental to a successful project. The emphasis is on much greater and more effective user involvement throughout the project life cycle.

SSADM and GUI Design: a Project Manager's Guide

In addition, there will need to be a powerful user presence on the project team to cover the specific requirements of end-users as well as user management. The project team must recognise the different roles to be played by representatives of end-users and user management. The direct involvement of end-users in GUI design is vital if the opportunities provided by GUI are to be exploited successfully.

The use of techniques such as prototyping alters the relationship between users and technical staff. There is far more contact; and users are included as part of the team rather than people with whom the project team have to deal. This increased involvement brings many benefits, but can also be the source of delay and uncontrolled iteration. Managers must be very careful to ensure that the ability to prototype and the satisfaction engendered are not allowed to run away with project timescales.

3.4.2 Team composition and responsibilities

New skills will be needed, particularly HCI analysis and design skills and experience of the chosen GUI. These will ensure that the real benefits of GUIs can be realised so that users are provided with systems which are easy to use and which make full use of the WIMP style of interface. Without these skills, there is a danger that laborious, character-based systems are replaced with equally laborious GUI equivalents.

The utilisation of different types of skill will change from the established profile for an SSADM project.

In order to retain control over GUI-based developments, it is common for a small team to be responsible for all GUI aspects. In a large team, it may be appropriate to identify a sub-team who are responsible for all GUI design; but care needs to be taken to ensure frequent communication with the other sub-team members. Managers will need to review carefully the scope and plans for individual activities, noting for example the earlier involvement of designers and programmers in building the system's GUI-prototype.

3.4.3   Training.   The development team will require training in the chosen GUI environment and the various additional techniques proposed for use with GUIs. This will need to be planned and scheduled within the overall project plan.

3.5   Implications for Project Management

3.5.1   Managing the process   Project management issues remain fundamentally the same; however, the process becomes somewhat more complex. The iterative nature of the approach must be accounted for by the manager when determining the completeness of a deliverable at the end of a step. At certain points, a number of different activities may progress in parallel and at greatly different speeds, increasing the need for good project management.

One project management option is to define much smaller blocks of work with smaller teams. There are many examples of organisations which do not allow complete projects or phases of work to exceed a few months in duration or occupy teams of more than 4 or 5 people.

For projects being managed under a PRINCE regime, some technical support in GUI Design could be provided by the Project Support Office (PSO); for example, the Technical Assurance Coordinator (TAC) could become the source of specialised technical guidance on the use of the GUI.

3.5.2   Quality Assurance   A natural corollary to management control issues is the difficulty of performing Quality Assurance (QA) reviews in the established way. The level of completeness for products expected at a particular iteration must be understood in terms of their extent or depth of information. Reviews must be adapted to cope with this situation, and an acceptable framework established for recording and tracking their move to full product description compliance over a longer period.

With a GUI environment, end-users have a much closer relationship with the system they are using, in that they will often dictate the way in which it is to be implemented. The greater use of screen based products will affect the QA procedures to be followed, as well as the testing strategies.

Some products, such as windows designs, are dynamic and are not easily committed to paper. Many will have quality criteria that depend on 'look and feel', therefore making them difficult to assure. In this context, it will be important to ensure such products comply with the agreed Installation and Application Style Guides.

3.5.3 Estimation

Experience is showing that the design of GUI systems will usually take as long, if not longer than that currently achieved for character screen based developments using the established core SSADM approach. The result should be a system more in tune with the needs of the end-user; and as a result of more effective analysis and design, it will require less modification of the user interface, and be considerably easier to enhance. But it will not be cheaper to develop.

User involvement places greater emphasis on the iterative nature of SSADM. This is particularly evident in the early stages of the project, when users may well be undertaking some of the tasks themselves; for example, the preparation of Task Scenarios and in the requirement for a considerably strengthened prototyping phase. This increases the uncertainties in planning the project, particularly in terms of estimation.

The balance of effort is also significantly changed:

- experience indicates that testing of GUI designs is likely to be more complex;

- in Stage 3, a large amount of effort will be devoted to user interface related activities, most of which will be concerned with Design, Prototype and Evaluate GUI (Step 365).

Planning and estimating workloads where a GUI is proposed is particularly difficult because there is still insufficient data to provide reliable metrics. These uncertainties increase the risk, and to offset this and the lack of data, PRINCE stages should be kept relatively short. Published metrics and estimating models for SSADM Version 4 will need to be reviewed and monitored in order to arrive at satisfactory guidance.

3.5.4 Procurement

One advantage of SSADM Version 4 is that it provides a sound basis for procurement, either through bespoke development or package acquisition.

The Stage 3 products of the SSADM Version 4 life-cycle provide a good, clean basis for developing an Operational Requirement on which a procurement can be based.

The iterative nature of GUI design makes the split between requirements specification and solution provision less clear. The problem is compounded by the fact that there is still relatively little experience of using an SSADM-based Operational Requirement to procure a solution that involves GUI design.

The basis of any procurement is to minimise risk and optimise value-for-money, without constraining suppliers to a particular solution. For purchasers in the public sector, there is an additional requirement to conform to GATT regulations as implemented within the European Community. These regulations will also apply to the private sector from 1 July 1994.

A key project management consideration for any SSADM and GUI project that involves procurement is to decide what SSADM products should be incorporated in the Operational Requirement, and what should be left to the supplier to develop.

The products developed in the tailored Stage 3 shown in Chapter 5 of this guide are one option for providing the basis of an Operational Requirement; but there are other options available.

As part of the project initiation process, the project manager must decide what SSADM and GUI products to include in the Operational Requirement, thereby deciding where the purchaser/supplier split will occur. The factors which will influence this decision will include level of risk, availability of package solutions, and the potential for incorporating prototypes as part of the ultimate solution.

4 Techniques and Products

4.1 Introduction

This chapter describes the additional techniques and products included in the tailored version of SSADM for GUI design. Including these techniques and products in a development will support a more user-centred approach to the design process, and provide an improved basis for GUI Design.

The level of description is targeted at describing what to do and not how to do it. References are provided which give descriptions of how each technique can be used.

4.1.1 What are these techniques?

The additional techniques come from many different sources, and have been integrated and tested within the HCI community.

User Analysis (4.2)

This builds on the existing SSADM User Catalogue, but extends it to cover the wide range of factors that need to influence GUI design. A detailed understanding of end-users is required to prevent developers seeing themselves as typical users.

Usability Analysis (4.3)

This expands on work on measuring and defining software quality, and applies the techniques to GUI development. It looks at refining the goals of the user interface and setting measurable criteria.

Task Modelling (4.4)

The origins of Task Modelling go back over twenty years in the human factors and training literature. It is an effective technique for modelling the activities that need to be performed from the users' perspective, and deciding with users which activities should be automated.

Task Scenario Definition (4.5)

This technique has been widely used informally, and is extended here to support task modelling and the design process.

Style Guide Definition (4.6)

Style Guides are described in SSADM. This section expands on the SSADM guidance, and describes how they can be used to support user interface consistency.

User Conceptual Modelling (4.7)

This technique has come out of human factors techniques, OO analysis, and data modelling. It is driven by the need for a higher level representation of a GUI design than that provided by screen layouts and connections.

GUI Design (4.8)

This draws from graphics design skills and knowledge of the interaction components in different GUI styles. It involves creating the visualisations and views that will support user tasks.

User Interface Prototyping (4.9)

User Interface Prototyping is needed in GUI to design good interfaces by watching users interact with prototypes early in the design process.

GUI Evaluation (4.10)

GUI Evaluation techniques are drawn from marketing, psychology, and HCI research. They support developers in identifying where the problems are in a user interface.

4.1.2 How do they fit together?

All these techniques are integrated into an effective approach for providing SSADM with the user centred design concepts for effective GUI design, as shown in the Product Flow Diagram in Figure 4-1. The integration with existing SSADM products is further defined in Chapters 5 and 6.

Chapter 4
Techniques and Products

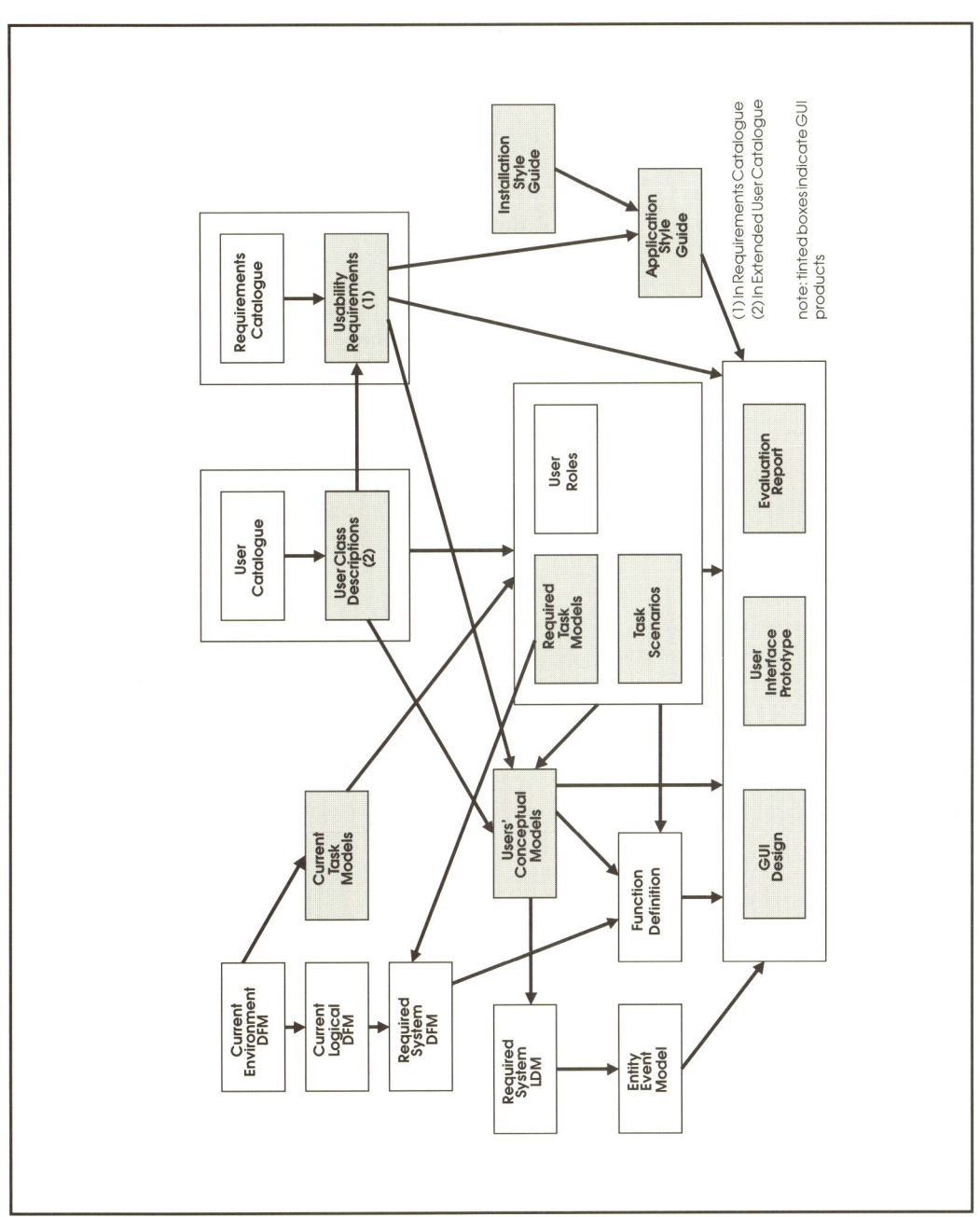

Figure 4-1: Product Flow Diagram

31

4.1.3 Presentation Structure for the Chapter

The description of each technique is split into the following sections:

Why do it?

Explains the rationale for the technique and why it is worth investing effort in it.

Description of Technique

Gives an overview of the technique in sufficient detail to understand what is involved in planning the project. It does not aim to explain how to perform the technique.

Inputs

Describes the different inputs to the technique or product.

Product

Describes what product or products the technique produces, where they are used, and the quality criteria that can be used to assess them.

Effort and skills

Gives guidance on how much effort will be required to perform the technique and the types of skills that are required.

Risks

Identifies common risks that need to be considered when performing the technique.

References

References papers and books detailed in the Bibliography that give further information on the technique.

4.2 User Analysis

4.2.1 Why do it?

The purpose of User Analysis is to understand the relevant characteristics of the population of end-users, in order to define usability requirements for that population.

System developers frequently assume that end-users will consider and interact with a GUI in the same way that developers do. Having an effective description of the skills and motivations of different types of users helps to guard against this.

A description of users is required to direct the process of GUI design to ensure that it can handle the range of user skills and capabilities identified. The technique also helps to identify why users need a new system, and the specific benefits which each group of users is seeking. It may be necessary to provide a different GUI presentation of a function because of the end-users' potential range of skills and capabilities.

Users with differing skills and capabilities may require different GUI presentations and even different system functionality to perform the same task. In SSADM terms, it may be important to design more than one variant of a function if it will be used by user classes with radically different levels of expertise. For example, word processing software may have a novice mode, and an expert mode which has additional functions and richer variants of the standard functions.

4.2.2 Description of Technique

The technique of User Analysis involves developing a description of the different users of the system, and how these users acquire skills in the use of the system over time. The first activity is to identify who the users of the new system will be from user jobs identified in the User Catalogue, and to classify these users into user classes. This is followed by identifying the characteristics of the users in each user class. The description needs to be in a form that motivates:

- the specification of usability requirements;
- design decisions.

SSADM and GUI Design: a Project Manager's Guide

The information can be collected through interviews with both managers and end-users, questionnaires, discussions with personnel departments, and observing users' work.

4.2.3   Inputs

The inputs to user analysis are:

- access to users
- sources of information about users
- User Catalogue

4.2.4   Product: User Class Descriptions

What it is

A user class is a subset of the total population of end-users of the required system, who are similar in terms of their frequency of use and relevant personal characteristics. The product consists of a report and a table that describes the user class.

It is often appropriate to divide the people in one job (as defined in the SSADM User Catalogue) into two or more user classes, depending on their pattern of use and personal characteristics or background. For example, the people who do the job of Benefits Clerk may be classified into three user classes: experienced continuous users; intermittent users; and trainees (i.e. novice users). The personal characteristics and usability requirements of the people in these user classes would then be considered separately.

This is illustrated in the example matrix in Figure 4-2.

Chapter 4
Techniques and Products

Job	User Classes		
Benefit Clerk	Clerk (Trainee)	Clerk (Intermittent)	Clerk (Experienced)
Sales Manager	Sales Manager (Inexperienced)		Sales Manager (Experienced)

Figure 4-2: User class matrix

User Class Descriptions are added to the (extended) User Catalogue.

For each user class, the description will include information on:

- type of access (direct/indirect/remote/support, etc.)
- frequency of use of system
- mandatory/discretionary use
- existing computer experience and skills
- education/intellectual abilities
- motivation for using the system and the specific goals
- numbers of users in each user class.

If relevant, it may also include information on differences between users:

- physical characteristics/capabilities
- language issues
- extent of task knowledge needed
- training they receive on systems
- organisational position
- how they are selected and promoted
- other systems that are used concurrently
- ways of working.

Where product is used	User Class Descriptions are used in a number of places, particularly to:

- define Usability Requirements for the most important user classes (Section 4.3);

- derive the Users' Conceptual Models, which depend on user background and pattern of use (Section 4.7);

- ensure that the Required Task Models are appropriate for these users (Section 4.4);

- develop Style Guides which support appropriate styles of interaction which are sensitive to characteristics, such as frequency of use (Section 4.6);

- create a suitable GUI Design which is harmonised with other systems used (Section 4.8);

- involve a good cross-section of users in GUI Evaluation, and ensure that the design meets their particular requirements (Section 4.10).

Quality Criteria	The quality criteria for User Class Descriptions are:

1. Is there sufficient information to guide analysis and design decisions?

2. Within each user class, are the characteristics and usability requirements similar? (If the system is usable by a few members of the user class who participate in user testing, is it reasonable to infer that it will be usable by the others?)

3. Have the numbers of users in each user class been identified?

4. Have the benefits of using the system been identified

Chapter 4
Techniques and Products

for each user class?

5. Have the implications for use been made explicit for each user class? For example: "because staff turnover is 40%, the training time must be less than 2 hours"; or "because half the staff can't read English well, all items must be recognisable by icons".

4.2.5	Effort and Skills	HCI analysis and design skills are valuable to identify relevant user characteristics and usability issues. The effort will be influenced by the population of users and the ease of identifying classes.
4.2.6	Risks	Risks to be avoided during User Analysis include:

- the description does not draw out the implications for GUI Design;

- time is wasted collecting information that is not pertinent to GUI Design;

- interviewing staff about their roles, motivation, etc. may be politically sensitive.

4.2.7 References HUFIT (1990)
Hix and Hartson (1993)

4.3 Usability Analysis

4.3.1 Why do it? Meeting Usability Requirements is critical to the success of a system. Usability criteria need to be set during the initial analysis phases of a GUI development. They can then be used subsequently to assess the quality of the user interface in terms of how well it supports user interaction. They should also be used during prototype evaluation to control and manage the prototyping and evaluation activities.

Systems are developed to meet business needs and provide business benefits. One way such benefits can be undermined by an otherwise functionally complete system is by failing to meet Usability Requirements.

Usability Requirements establish capabilities and qualities for user interface designs. During design, these requirements are used to assess the design as it develops, and as a basis for making trade-offs between alternative design options.

Usability Requirements stated in terms of criteria permit the usability of a system to be tested. In this way, the procurer of a system can establish measures by which the required system can be assessed.

The usability criteria will be used during the evaluation of prototype(s) and provide a basis for prioritising requested changes to the prototype.

4.3.2 Description of Technique

Usability Requirements should be identified during the analysis phases of a project, particularly Stage 1 of SSADM.

Usability Requirements are documented as statements such as: "operators should only require a one hour training course before they can use 90% of the functionality of a system without recourse to supporting documentation". When documenting such requirements, the analyst must ensure that they are measurable. If they cannot be measured, they are of no value.

Usability criteria are usually drawn from one of the following categories:

Productivity
Learnability
User satisfaction
Memorability
Error rates.

For convenience, these categories are referred to as the **PLUME** metrics. Usability Requirements have to be stated in terms of tasks, and should be related to User Class Descriptions. For instance, there might be a requirement associated with a billing system that states: "invoicing clerks having completed their training course should be able to process 30 invoices per hour with the new system, and with an error rate of less than one per

Chapter 4
Techniques and Products

hundred invoices". A further example might be: "managers should judge the system on average as 2, on a rating scale in which 1 signified complete satisfaction and 7 complete dissatisfaction".

4.3.3 Inputs

Usability Requirements may be identified at any point during the analysis and design phases of a project. The most fruitful sources of Usability Requirements are:

- usability of the existing system, which represents a baseline level of usability for the replacement system;

- relevant human factors literature, which provides much information on metrics and how they might be measured;

- expected business benefits, for example, to reduce the level of staff turnover, reduce training times, etc;

- the investigative steps of task modelling;

- User Class Description;

- Requirements Catalogue.

4.3.4 Product: Usability Requirements

What it is

Usability Requirements are statements regarding the needs of users when interacting with a system. Statements can take two forms. Firstly, they can refer to facilities or capabilities that the system must provide. These might include undo-redo facilities, or fastpaths for experienced users. Secondly, they may set usability criteria, for instance that users should be able to process twenty customer enquiries an hour. Usability Requirements are captured in the Requirements Catalogue.

Given the importance of Requirements Analysis in general, it is felt that undertaking Usability Analysis is worthwhile, even if there is overlap between products. Indeed, Usability Analysis not only contributes to the

SSADM and GUI Design: a Project Manager's Guide

Requirements Catalogue, but it also provides a check on its quality and completeness.

Usability Requirements will be documented as additions to the Requirements Catalogue. For convenience, they may be indexed separately.

Usability Requirements will be stated in terms of:

- tasks to which they relate
- criteria to be met where applicable
- source (where or how identified) of the requirement
- business benefits to which they contribute
- user classes to which they apply.

Where product is used

Usability Requirements are used in a number of places to drive and control user interface design. In particular, they are used to:

- evaluate the GUI Design in advance of end-user evaluation (Section 4.8);

- structure interactive evaluations of prototypes within GUI Evaluation (Section 4.10);

- support acceptance testing;

- develop the Application Style Guide (Section 4.6);

- during the final acceptance testing of the product.

Quality Criteria

The quality criteria for Usability Requirements are:

1. Are all usability criteria measurable?

2. Have the usability criteria been related to User Class Descriptions and their tasks?

3. Are the Usability Requirements sufficiently comprehensible to both users and their management?

4. Have business benefit(s) been related to the usability criteria?

Chapter 4
Techniques and Products

4.3.5	Effort and Skills	There needs to be a mix of business and HCI analysis and design skills involved in this process:

- business skills are required to identify the business benefits arising from improved usability;

- HCI skills are required to identify Usability Requirements during analysis, and ensure that reasonable usability criteria are specified.

The effort required to develop Usability Requirements will be dependent on the value of business benefits derived from improved usability. Collecting all the data required to quantify current usability can be time consuming, but allows the setting of measurable targets.

4.3.6	Risks	The following risks to setting and meeting Usability Requirements need to be noted:

- impractical usability criteria are set: Usability Requirements must be achievable, given the constraints of a project;

- the usability criteria do not contribute to business benefits, making them of questionable value;

- the usability criteria are ignored during prototype evaluation.

4.3.7	References	Helander (1988) Browne (1994) ISO TC159/SC4/WG5 (1990)

4.4 Task Modelling

4.4.1	Why do it?	Task Modelling is concerned with analysing, documenting, and designing users' tasks. It is needed to provide a user description of activities, and ensure that the user interface supports the users' tasks.

An understanding of the users' tasks in an application area provides designers with information about what a system will be used for and how it will be used. It shows the mappings that are necessary to go from a specific user goal to a set of actions to perform that goal. Without this important understanding, user requirements can be missed, unnecessary complexity built in, and effort often wasted in developing excessive system functionality.

<table>
<tr><td>4.4.2 Description of Technique</td><td>Task Modelling provides techniques for analysing, documenting and designing users' tasks. A rapid Task Model can be developed to explore design alternatives and a more detailed model can look at performance issues and identify potential user errors. This activity is similar to process analysis, but takes an end user's perspective.</td></tr>
</table>

During analysis, two variants of the Task Model will be produced: the Current Task Model; and the Required Task Model. A high level DFD can be used to scope and drive the Current Task Model. The Required Task Model is derived from an understanding of how current tasks can be removed or simplified.

A task is an activity which has identified start and end points that are meaningful to users. A task can be defined as the job users are trying to do, such as sending a message, logging on to a remote database, or entering an order. Tasks are performed to meet some goal which itself can be part of a hierarchy of goals. If a user's goal is to arrange a meeting, this can be broken down into a number of tasks, such as finding a room, and setting a date; each of which can be further described and analysed. The analysis is performed on current tasks and then abstracted and mapped onto future task demands.

During Task Modelling, user terms should be collected into a Glossary, and options for allocating functions to users and system can be considered and reviewed.

<table>
<tr><td>Allocation of tasks to user and system</td><td>The allocation of tasks needs to be considered throughout Stage 3, and is concerned with identifying which tasks should be done by the system and which by the user. This can be started once an initial task analysis has been performed.</td></tr>
</table>

Identifying information requirements	This involves identifying the decisions that users take at particular points in the tasks and the information they require to make those decisions. This activity feeds into the identification of the Users' Conceptual Model.
Tasks and Functions	Task Models are related to SSADM Function Definitions in the following way: During task allocation, the Task Model is divided between what the user does, and one or more processes performed by the system. There are often design alternatives in how this system processing should be organised and presented to the user in terms of SSADM Functions. The relationship between tasks and SSADM Functions is many-to-many. A simple task typically requires one function. A complex task may require several functions. One function may be used in the context of many different tasks.

4.4.3 Inputs

Inputs to the development of a Task Model can include:

- interviews with users
- observations of users performing tasks
- any written procedures
- Current Data Flow Model.

In addition, for the Required Task Model:

- Task Scenarios
- User Class Descriptions

These may be supplemented by users commenting on task structures and reviews.

4.4.4 Product: Task Model

What it is

The Task Model is a hierarchical description with supporting notes. This should include:

- user goals
- task frequency
- which User Roles perform which tasks.

Where product is used

The Current Task Model is abstracted and generalised, and is used to feed into the Required Task Model. In particular, it helps to identify:

- problems in the current task;
- areas where end-users require more support;
- options for allocation of functions between user and system (Business System Options);
- areas of complexity in the task.

The Required Task Model is used to:

- help identify different User Roles;
- provide a user oriented input to Function Definition;
- derive and validate the Users' Conceptual Model by helping to identify objects and actions required by users in performing identified tasks (Section 4.7).

Task frequency information is used to determine where to focus design effort, and look for cost-effective performance improvements.

Quality Criteria

The quality criteria for Task Modelling are:

1. Is there outline coverage (not more than four levels deep) of the current user tasks, and more detailed descriptions of the required tasks?

2. Have the pre-conditions for performing a task been reduced to a minimum?

3. Is there a clear task goal?

4. Has the task structure been validated with users?

5. Is it clear what information is required to perform the task and what information is produced as a result?

6. Does the user have this information available?

7. What external events, related tasks, volumetric/timing data is associated with this task, and has all the

information been collected and documented?

8. Have all the User Roles and devices involved in the task been identified?

4.4.5 Effort and Skills

It is often not necessary for all user tasks to be fully analysed and formally documented. Most effort should be devoted to the tasks which are critical in some way; for example, tasks which are frequent, difficult, require fast performance, must have few errors, or must have high usability. For some lower profile tasks, task analysis may be performed informally, with the resulting Task Models being internal working documents rather than formal products. For very simple tasks with simple functionality where usability is not a major issue, the project manager may decide to omit task analysis. Usability for these tasks, where appropriate, is validated by users during prototyping.

The skills required to perform task analysis are those of a good analyst who can understand what the user is doing and why, and document that in the appropriate notation.

4.4.6 Risks

The following risks need to be considered during Task Modelling:

- the task structure can be built in such a way that it does not match the user's view of how the task is performed;

- each user performs the task differently;

- the current task structure is constrained by existing forms or processes, and does not provide an effective basis for considering the required task;

- too much time is wasted analysing and reviewing the tasks in great detail, and Task Modelling becomes an end in itself;

- stakeholders worry that they are losing control when analysts talk directly to end-users.

4.4.7 References

Diaper (1989)

Browne (1994)

4.5 Task Scenario Definition

4.5.1 Why do it?

The development of scenarios for specific user tasks provides a number of benefits for a project, such as:

- helping to provide realistic examples and test cases;

- developing and validating the Required Task Models (Section 4.4);

- providing a common set of examples that can be used to integrate different parts of the project;

- supporting improved communication with users;

- allowing realistic prototypes to be set up, based on the Task Scenarios, which increases the effectiveness of user evaluation.

These benefits, and the low level of effort required to develop Task Scenarios, makes them a very cost effective addition to the development process.

4.5.2 Description of Technique

Task Scenario development is the collection of representative sets of actions and parameters providing examples of task completion.

The process involves the following steps:

- scope the type and number of Task Scenarios to collect, and which users performed them;

- determine level of detail and method of documenting;

- collect and document Task Scenarios from users;

- review to check that they are representative.

4.5.3 Inputs

The inputs to the Task Scenario Definition technique are:

- User Catalogue;
- Task Model.

4.5.4   Product: Task Scenarios

What it is

A Task Scenario is a concrete example of a specific path through a task (or set of tasks) which provides a complete story. This technique produces a report which contains a list of Task Scenarios. A Task Scenario describes the actions that a user will perform in using the system to achieve some goal or respond to an event. This report should also contain either measured or estimated figures of the frequency of the task of which the Task Scenario is an example, and the importance of being able to deal with the task. This information will feed into the usability specification.

Where product is used

Task Scenarios are used for the following:

- as input to Task Modelling and as a way of validating the Required Task Models that are developed (Section 4.4);

- to support communication among the development team and to enhance communication with users;

- to validate the Function Definitions and the Users' Conceptual Models (Section 4.7);

- as a way of validating the GUI Design (Section 4.8);

- as input and example data for User Interface Prototyping (Section 4.9).

An understanding of the Task Scenarios can be used to drive the user interface design and act as a focus for discussing different interface designs.

Quality Criteria

The quality criteria for Task Scenarios are:

1. Are the Task Scenarios representative of the types of situation that users have to deal with, including common operations, system failures, and some

exceptional cases?

2. Has the importance of each Task Scenario been defined quantitatively?

3. Has the expected frequency of occurrence of each Task Scenario type been defined?

4. Have the Task Scenarios been validated by users other than those who provided them?

5. Is sufficient information provided to ensure that the Task Scenarios are understandable by the project team?

4.5.5 Effort and Skills

Task Scenario definition requires good analytic skills to understand and document the scenarios at an appropriate level to support the design process.

The effort involved depends on the number of Task Scenarios that are developed, their complexity, and how they are validated.

4.5.6 Risks

The following risks may exist whilst developing Task Scenarios:

- the scenarios collected may be unrepresentative of the actual usage of the system;

- developers focus on the most complex scenarios, and ignore the 80% which are the day to day tasks.

4.5.7 References

Hix and Hartson (1993)
Gould, Boies, Levy, Richards, and Scoonard (1990)

4.6 Style Guide Definition

4.6.1 Why do it?

The reasons for developing an **Installation Style Guide** are to:

- improve consistency of the user interfaces across applications to enable application integration,

Chapter 4
Techniques and Products

increase user productivity, and allow staff mobility;

- reduce users' training time by achieving consistency within and across applications;

- prevent developers from re-inventing all aspects of the user interface, and allow them to concentrate on application-specific details.

The reasons for developing an **Application Style Guide** are to:

- improve consistency of an application's user interface as it is being developed rather than trying to build in consistency at systems integration;

- agree and document a common 'look-and-feel' to the user interface, so that the design can be carried out by different people;

- promote good design practice across the development team;

- ensure compliance with appropriate user interface standards and regulations.

4.6.2 Description of Technique

An Installation Style Guide is often developed at the same time as the first GUI-based development. This technique builds on the procedures described in the Version 4 Manuals.

The development of an Installation Style Guide involves identifying a suitable base standard, such as IBM's Common User Access, OSF/Motif, or Microsoft's Windows, that is appropriate to the target platform. These standards are generic, and need to be enhanced to address the specific areas of concern for the installation.

An Installation Style Guide can include:

- the type of applications for which the Style Guide is applicable;

- specific development principles (such as when and where to use a modal style) for the user interface;

- common facilities all applications should support;

- navigation standards for moving around the application;

- keyboard standards for common functions;

- user interface components to use, and rules for selecting them;

- naming standards, symbols, and data formats;

- standard window layouts;

- organisation of the help system;

- conformance checklist and procedures.

The process of producing an Application Style Guide should build on the Installation Style Guide. The guidance in an Installation Style Guide will often need to be made more specific for a project. An Application Style Guide can include:

- any modifications to the Installation Style Guide, together with a justification;

- specific words that will be used in the interface, and a definition;

- details of any custom controls;

- specific layouts and formats that will be used;

- details of new uses of control keys.

4.6.3 Inputs

The inputs to the development of an Installation Style Guide are:

- existing commercial Style Guides such as OSF/Motif, IBM's Common User Access, and

Microsoft's Windows Style Guide;

- relevant external literature on standards such as ISO 9241, guidelines, and user interface design books;

- details of users and their tasks;

- details of the types of application being developed.

The inputs to the development of an Application Style Guide are:

- existing Installation Style Guide;

- constraints and features of development tools;

- details of the application;

- Usability Requirements.

4.6.4 Product: Installation Style Guide

What it is

The Installation Style Guide is a document which defines the consistency standards that will be followed by the user interfaces of a range of applications. It needs to include:

- standards for the user interface and some supporting rationale;

- guidance material for educating developers;

- a conformance checklist for critical areas of the standard;

- an explanation of the overall structure and framework for an application.

Where product is used

The Installation Style Guide is used to document the standard that should be adopted by all new applications. It should be developed prior to the first GUI development. It should be used:

- to develop the Application Style Guide;
- during the procurement process to select software;
- at review stages to check consistency;
- during compliance testing to ensure that the interface is consistent.

4.6.5 Product: Application Style Guide

What it is

The Application Style Guide is a project-specific document which defines the consistency standards that will be followed during user interface development. It documents the areas of agreement that have been reached on a project, and any justified changes to the Installation Style Guide. It needs to include:

- specific project standards for the user interface that take into account the constraints of the implementation tool;

- a conformance checklist for critical areas of the standard;

- detailed naming and layout standards.

Where product is used

The Application Style Guide is developed ahead of the initial prototypes and is then refined and updated on an agreed basis. It can also be used during:

- initial GUI Design to ensure that consistent interfaces are developed (Section 4.8);

- integration to check consistency;

- compliance testing to ensure that the interface is consistent.

Quality Criteria

The quality criteria for Style Guides are:

1. Are the Style Guides applicable and implementable in the target environment?

2. Are the Style Guides clear and unambiguous to developers?

3. Is the organisation and structure of each guide such that readers can rapidly find the relevant information?

4. Have sufficient pictures and examples been included?

5. Is the style described appropriate for users' tasks?

6. Do the guides differentiate between mandatory and optional style rules?

4.6.6 Effort and Skills

The development of an Installation Style Guide can take between one and three months. Much of this effort goes on understanding the environment, developing effective examples, and getting agreement on the Style Guide from the many interested parties.

The effort to develop an Application Style Guide depends on the complexity of the environment, the starting point, and the sophistication of the user interface. Much of this effort goes on documenting and getting agreement on the standards.

The skills required are a user interface developer who is familiar with Style Guides and has some knowledge of the development environment.

4.6.7 Risks

The following risks need to be addressed during the development of Style Guides, which can:

- remain unfinished and not signed off before development starts, and be ignored;

- stay very generic, and provide no specific standards above the existing commercial style guides;

- become extremely detailed, and even include the code for implementing a specific feature, which should be kept in a reusable style library;

- be unaccepted by developers, so that conformance checks are never carried out;

- contain arbitrary decisions with no rationale; for

example, menus shall contain between five and nine actions;

- fail to be implementable in the target environment.

4.6.8 References CCTA (1991a) and (1991b)
Apple Computer Inc (1992)
IBM (1991)
OSF/MOTIF (1993)
Microsoft (1992)
Nielsen (1989)

4.7 User Conceptual Modelling

4.7.1 Why do it? User Conceptual Modelling is used to identify the information which should be presented, what relationships are important to users, and the rules and relationships that should be preserved in the interface. It is needed to develop an effective organisation of the GUI which makes it easy for end-users to learn and control the system.

A User Conceptual Model is, in essence, an end-user's mental model of the structure and contents of the system, which identifies simple mapping rules that allow the end-user to predict how the system operates.

Ensuring that a coherent and appropriate Users' Conceptual Model is 'designed in' to the GUI will promote system usability. Note that the Users' Conceptual Model must not be confused with the SSADM Conceptual Model described in Chapter 6.

4.7.2 Description of Technique The analyst must identify whether variations between jobs are so great that multiple Users' Conceptual Models are required (e.g. one for clerks, another for accountants).

It is important to identify, analyse and develop a model for what the end-user will think is 'in the system' and how it is structured and organised. What you are trying to do is identify the 'things in the system' the end-users believe they are seeing and interacting with in the

Chapter 4
Techniques and Products

interface. These 'things in the system' are sometimes referred to as 'objects'; but this is a loose use of the term, and not to be confused with the encapsulated objects in an object-oriented programming language.

The objects and actions in the Users' Conceptual Model should be selected and defined to support the users' tasks, as defined in the Required Task Model and Task Scenarios.

The purpose of the Users' Conceptual Model is to answer questions such as: 'which things do the users think of as 'close' to each other, or related to each other?' 'Is there a sense of up/down or north/south or inside/outside?' 'What sense of context or direction do they have; and how, in general, do they navigate?'

User Conceptual Modelling is rather subtle; and three approaches which are sometimes appropriate are:

1. Basing the Users' Conceptual Model on the SSADM Logical Data Model and Entity-Event Model. This can involve:

- collapsing entities with their masters (e.g. an 'order' in the Users' Conceptual Model will usually represent at least two entities in the LDM);

- splitting entities back into the 1:1 relationships which disappeared in data modelling;

- recording different relationships which are important to the user.

The user will not be aware of the complexity of Enquiry Access Paths; just of the results of enquiries.

There is also a need to record:

- the behaviour of these 'user entities';

- useful pictorial concepts discovered during user analysis and task analysis.

2. The Users' Conceptual Model can be framed within some analogy or metaphor. Examples include:

- the familiar 'desktop' metaphor;

- a map metaphor with 'zoom in';

- a 'book' metaphor for a hypertext system (contents list, chapters, index, etc.);

- a typewriter metaphor for a word processor.

Metaphors can be helpful for behaviour and spatial organisation, but often do not represent the relationships between objects very well.

3. The production of a 'user object model'. This consists of the objects, actions, attributes, and relationships between objects in the system as perceived by the end-user. Note that behaviour (ie functionality) is an integral part of these objects. Diagram notations such as object-relationship models can be used to represent the structure of objects. The user will see 'views' or visualisations of these objects in the interface.

In User Conceptual Modelling, there is a move from analysis: "what concepts does the user use now?" to design of the required system: "what concepts will be helpful to the user in the new system?"

The Users' Conceptual Model is documented as a design for the end-user's mental model. The team should produce and review a glossary of user terms for the objects, actions, and relationships visible to the user. The terms derived should be incorporated within the Application Style Guide.

The 'objects' in the Users' Conceptual Model and their relationships are mapped back to the Logical Data Model, extending the LDM if required.

The team must consider whether there are powerful visualisations of objects in the Users' Conceptual Model, that can be used in the system image to support users in their tasks and facilitate user comprehension.

User Conceptual Modelling is shown as a distinct step in the Structural Model to emphasise its importance. However, some of the activities described might take place in other steps.

4.7.3 Inputs

Inputs to User Conceptual Modelling include:

- user interviews, to identify pre-existing Users' Conceptual Models;

- models of the problem domain, specifically the Logical Data Model;

- User Class Descriptions;

- Required Task Model, which provides:
  - understanding of the users' tasks;
  - identification of the decisions that users make;
  - definition of information and feedback needed to support user tasks.

4.7.4 Product: Users' Conceptual Model

What it is

The Users' Conceptual Model can be a composite product. The user object model, for example, would consist of the Object Model, Data Model Cross Reference, Object-Action Matrix, and Glossary.

Object Model

A model of the objects and relationships in the system, as understood by the user. This describes the underlying objects presented to users, the actions that users can perform on these objects, and the attributes they have. The objects need to be simple for the users to understand, and to support users' tasks. The actions are defined in terms of the effect they have on the system (e.g. output caused, processing activated, data created or updated).

For example, in an electronic mail system, 'message' is an important object, and the user expects to perform such 'actions' on it as edit, send, delete, copy, etc.

Similarly, in a sales order processing system, 'sales order' is an important object, including the sales order lines (a repeating group), and the user expects to perform actions such as create, check-credit, invoice, cancel. 'Enquiry' might be a separate object, in spite of the fact that there is a one-to-one relationship with sales order (many enquiries turn into orders). The point here is that we are adopting the viewpoint of end-users, who think of enquiries and orders as different objects, with different attributes and actions; rather than the viewpoint of data modellers, who would collapse the one-to-one relationship into a single entity.

Some of the 'objects' in the object model correspond to entities, but in general the model differs from a Logical Data Model in several ways:

- some objects are not entities at all, e.g. artifacts such as documents or printers or mailboxes (that would not be stored in the database at all); or collections or containers such as schedules or catalogues, (which may be derived from multiple stored entity occurrences);

- many of the objects are composites which are not even approximately normalised (e.g. they may have multi-valued attributes). For example, the whole of a benefit application form could be one object;

- some of the objects have a very rich structure, and are best viewed as a diagram, plan, or map;

- many-to-many and one-to-one relationships are common.

Data Model Cross-Reference

A mapping of the information content (attributes) of the object model to the logical data model. This ensures that the user's view can be supported by the data model where appropriate.

Object-Action Matrix

This shows which actions affect which objects in the model, and how. It is used to check the consistency of the Users' Conceptual Model.

Glossary

A definitive list of the user terms which will be used in the interface, with their meanings. Most of these are names of objects, relationships, attributes, actions, states of objects, or rules about actions or objects. The glossary may be contained in the Application Style Guide.

Where product is used	The Users' Conceptual Model is used to:

- identify and specify Function Definitions to meet users' task requirements, from actions on objects.

- organise GUI Design, where windows contain views of objects in the Users' Conceptual Model. The glossary guides the phrasing of all labels, menus, messages, etc (Section 4.8).

- evaluate the GUI design and prototype in terms of whether they support (or clash with) the Users' Conceptual Model (Section 4.10).

Quality Criteria	The quality criteria for each Users' Conceptual Model are:

1. Task Support: does the Users' Conceptual Model have the right objects and actions, and make the right information visible, to support the Required Task Model?

2. Completeness: are all the objects, actions, attributes, relationships, and terms required by these users included in the model and the glossary?

3. Will each object be amenable to (one or more) visualisations which show its capabilities and encourage the right user behaviour?

4. Is the Users' Conceptual Model unnecessarily rich for

SSADM and GUI Design: a Project Manager's Guide

users who only need to perform simple tasks? (In other words, can more information and functionality be safely hidden?)

5. Will the model be recognisable and meaningful to users in the relevant user class(es)? Have existing user concepts and terminology been retained (and built upon where appropriate)?

6. Do the models provide a consistent view of the system's facilities as users progress from novice to expert?

7. Can users successfully predict the operation of a new part of the system from their knowledge of an existing part?

8. Does the glossary contain different terms for the same thing, or very similar terms for different things, which are likely to lead to confusion?

9. Do the models achieve coverage of the Required Logical Data Model? (i.e. all the entities, relationships, and data items should be used by or visible in at least one of the models).

Integration with SSADM V4 Products

The Users' Conceptual Model is used to structure the user interface. Figure 4-3 shows schematically how a user sees and interacts with 'objects in the system' by actions on views of those objects displayed in windows. The user's actions are translated into the events and enquiries which form the substance of underlying system functionality, and access stored data. The results of the events and enquiries are translated back into the GUI images in the interface.

Designing a Users' Conceptual Model is concerned with choices of how to organise system functionality (events and enquiries) into a collection of related objects which will be meaningful to the users and useful for their tasks.

The SSADM Entity-Event Model, on the other hand, is concerned with creating a logical view of the system data, and the events and enquiries which access that data.

Chapter 4
Techniques and Products

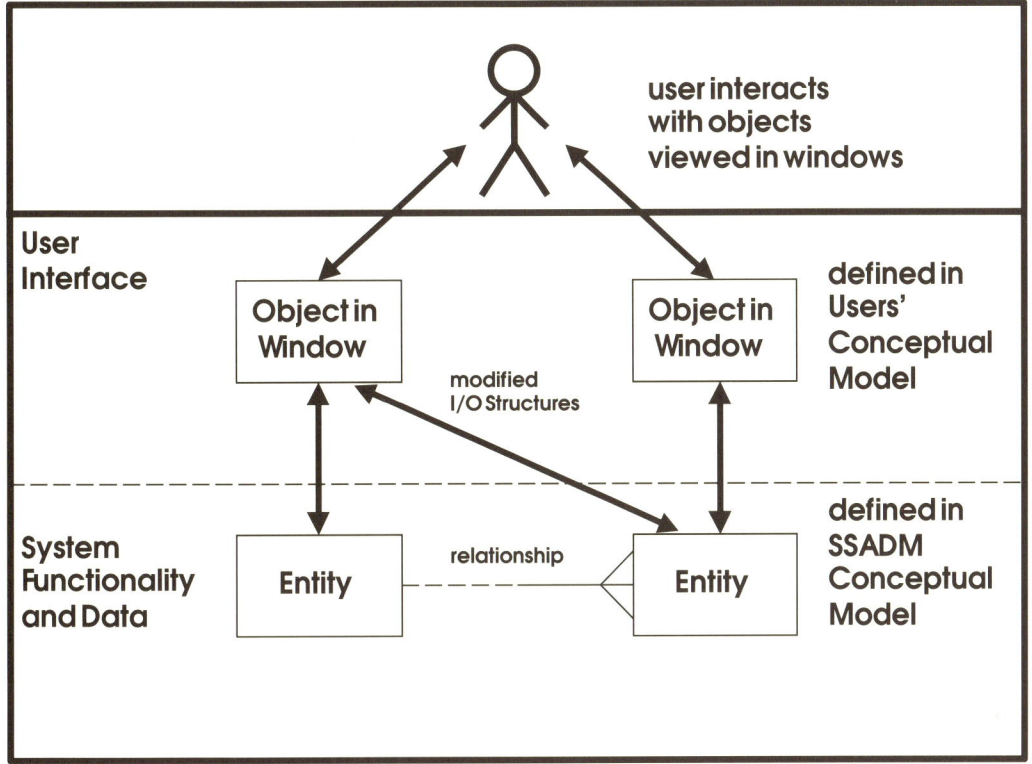

Figure 4-3: The Role of the Users' Conceptual Model

4.7.5 Effort and Skills   This is a subtle area where HCI analysis and design skills are particularly valuable.

Access to end-users for elicitation of existing Users' Conceptual Models and validation of a proposed model is important.

If there are more than 30 objects, effort should be expended in trying to reduce the number of objects that the user needs to understand.

4.7.6 Risks   The risk in User Conceptual Modelling is the production

61

of a complex analytical model which cannot be realistically implemented, and/or would not be comprehensible to the end-user.

4.7.7 References

Norman (1988)
Open University (1990)
Hix and Hartson (1993)
IBM (1991)

4.8 GUI Design

4.8.1 Why do it?

To create a GUI Design which:

- supports user tasks;

- is comprehensible to the user by reflecting the intended Users' Conceptual Model;

- is consistent in style by conforming to the Application Style Guide.

The technique assists in achieving a reasonable initial GUI Design, which is input to a process of prototyping and evaluation.

It also contributes to producing a final GUI Design, which is a substantial part of the Required System Specification agreed at the end of Stage 3.

4.8.2 Description of Technique

The Users' Conceptual Model defines objects that the end-user thinks are 'in the system'. GUI Design is concerned with:

- defining views and visualisations of these objects;

- designing windows based on these views;

- mapping Function Definition input/output into windows

- assembling the windows together into a well-structured user interface that supports user tasks, and helps the user to use Functions effectively.

Chapter 4
Techniques and Products

This activity is concerned with design rather than analysis. Consequently, there is usually no single correct answer: there are frequently several quite different design solutions, each of which may be acceptable. The Usability Requirements form a basis on which to limit the choice of design solutions. Creativity, lateral thinking, and breadth of experience will frequently play a part in this process.

The technique is applied in three phases:

- Initial GUI Design. Creates a 'first-cut' GUI Design that can be used to start the process of prototyping and evaluation.

- Refinement of GUI Design. Design evolves through prototyping. The aim is to modify and add to the design by reference to the user, task refinement and usability evolution, whilst retaining coherence and consistency.

- Finalisation of GUI Design. Omissions and defects are resolved and consistency ensured.

The technique commonly includes the following design activities:

- views of objects required for user tasks are identified;

- views of objects are allocated to windows, taking account of the Application Style Guide, and the objects, attributes and actions are allocated to window controls;

- I/O Structures within Function Definitions are mapped onto windows, identifying common windows and/or processing common to more than one Function;

- user interface interaction is designed for each of the actions in the Users' Conceptual Model and for each Function; for example, pull-down controls, secondary windows or dialogue boxes, and other interface components;

- window navigation is designed, based on the relationships in the Users' Conceptual Model;

- Task Scenarios are 'walked through' to ensure that windows are usable for user tasks, and that all the required navigation paths have been defined.

As the design progresses and issues are resolved, both the Users' Conceptual Model and the Application Style Guide may be revised. Function Definitions may also be revised.

The technique produces a GUI Design, including initial error messages, outline help subsystem, etc.

4.8.3   Inputs

Inputs to GUI Design include:

- User Class Descriptions;
- Usability Requirements;
- Users' Conceptual Models;
- Required Task Models;
- Task Scenarios;
- Application Style Guide;
- Function Definitions;
- Entity-Event Model (the GUI provides a user interface to events).

4.8.4   Product: GUI Design

What it is

The main components of GUI Design are:

- list of windows, and any other interface components (e.g. desktop, icons, top menu, log-in sequence);

- window designs for each window, its layout, visual contents, the interface actions the user can perform on it, a definition of the effect of each action, and the conditions under which it can be used (eg greying conditions);

Chapter 4
Techniques and Products

- window navigation design, comprising diagram(s) and other documentation defining how the user reaches all parts of the interface, and moves between one representation and another;

- GUI Design/Function/Event Cross-reference, a definition of which interface actions are associated with (i.e. invoke) which Functions and events.

Where product is used Evolving GUI Designs are the starting point for various kinds of evaluation and testing:

- during User Interface Prototyping for the development of a software prototype followed by user testing (Section 4.9);

- during GUI Evaluation for analytical evaluation, Task Scenarios or design metrics, and for storyboard evaluation with the user (Section 4.10);

- during Physical Design, where the components of the GUI Design are linked to the processing specifications in Step 650.

Quality Criteria The quality criteria for the GUI Design are:

1. Is the design simple and flexible?

2. How well does the design support the tasks the user needs to perform?

3. Can the end-user interpret what the representation means easily and correctly, relate it to their tasks, and understand any feedback they receive?

4. To what extent does the design convey and conform to the intended Users' Conceptual Model?

5. Does the GUI Design conform to the Application Style Guide?

6. Is all the GUI Design necessary to perform user tasks and support the Users' Conceptual Model?

7. Does the GUI Design satisfy the agreed Usability Requirements?

8. Is the GUI Design sufficiently detailed, complete, and unambiguous that it can form an adequate specification of future development work?

9. Does the GUI Design contain all help and error messages?

10. Can all required Functions be called from the GUI? Does the GUI deal with all Function input, output, and control?

11. Is the design implementable in the chosen GUI environment?

4.8.5 Effort and Skills

Designing a Graphical User Interface is more complex, and typically takes more effort than character-based screen design for a system with equivalent business functionality. GUI Design experience and skill is important.

Estimating the time for GUI Design will depend on the number of custom components that need to be developed, and the complexity of the windows and navigation options.

Additional effort will be required to check consistency, look at integration issues, and to finalise the component design.

4.8.6 Risks

The risks involved in GUI Design are:

- too much effort is invested in trying to reach a perfect design before the users see it, followed by a reluctance to evolve it;

- an inappropriate initial GUI Design, resulting in evaluation and redesign based on the wrong start point;

- use of too many 'clever' features, confusing the user;

- specification of multiple features that make the design excessively expensive to develop and test.

4.8.7	References	IBM (1991) Hix and Hartson (1993) Open University (1990)

4.9 User Interface Prototyping

4.9.1	Why do it?	The Graphical User Interface has dynamic properties which are often difficult, if not impossible, to convey via text. A prototype is a working example of the system, or a subset of it, which allows the users and the developers to interact with it. Through this interaction, the prototype allows the project to:

- identify user requirements;

- refine incomplete and ambiguous requirements;

- validate requirements early in the design when changes can be made cost effectively;

- test alternative design options for critical areas;

- get feedback on user interface design and Style Guide issues in order to improve the system's usability.

4.9.2	Description of Technique	User Interface Prototyping is not recommended as a method of systems development; rather it is a technique that can be used within the systems development process. After a prototype has been developed, it can be demonstrated or evaluated, and the result fed into the next stage of development or used to modify the prototype further. It provides an effective way of learning, identifying and resolving problems. It is also a good technique to support Requirements Specification, hence its inclusion in Stage 3.

The reader is referred to the CCTA publication *Prototyping within an SSADM Environment* (1993) as a good source of information on the role of prototyping within SSADM.

User Interface Prototyping involves developing a mock-up of the user interface. This mock-up must be sufficiently realistic to enable valid and reliable evaluations to be performed. Given that a user interface should be considered as including all user documentation and peripherals (such as phones), these should be treated as integral aspects of a prototype wherever they play a role in the users' tasks. The complexity of this mock-up will vary depending on the application area and the purpose of the prototype.

The demonstration of User Interface Prototypes needs to be carefully controlled, because they can often create false expectations. Sometimes the end-users, and their management, are left with the impression that the system is complete, or nearing completion, rather than just a mock-up.

A technical review of the prototype should be carried out before it is tested by users, to ensure that the concepts demonstrated are technically feasible within the project budget.

The scope of the User Interface Prototype needs to be controlled to ensure that the prototype development meets its objectives. For example, if the scope of the prototype is not defined, the project can put more and more functionality into the GUI prototype until it provides the same functionality as the required system. In addition, when used iteratively in conjunction with evaluation techniques, the whole process needs to be controlled to ensure that costs and timescales do not rise inordinately.

Iteration is a necessary aspect of prototyping. For project managers, iteration is a sensitive issue, because it can often be difficult to control and predict. There must be a prototyping plan to manage this iteration. This plan must include statements of objectives to be met by the prototype. There are also a number of techniques, including impact analysis, for controlling iteration. Impact analysis, as referred to here, relies on quantifying the expected benefits of making changes to the prototype, quantifying the costs of those changes, and on these bases choosing which changes to make. In this way, impact analysis ensures that limited resources are deployed to best effect, or until all usability criteria have been met.

Setting a limit on the number of iterations round the prototype-evaluate cycle is not enough, as this will not control the costs and timescales of each iteration. In addition, setting a limit to the number of iterations implies that each iteration must be performed, when in fact occasions will arise when it makes no sense to perform all the iterations: for example, when all the usability criteria have been met. It is far better to control iterative prototyping on the basis of attainment of usability criteria. There may, however, be occasions when it is found that it is not possible to meet all usability criteria. On such occasions, a compromise will have to be found in order to produce a system within the cost constraints of the project.

Project documentation is an important part of the prototyping process which is often overlooked. User Interface Prototyping is a process rather than a product, and it is important that the process is documented. This documentation provides a trail of the user interface design, including a note of those things which met Usability Requirements and those which did not.

4.9.3 Inputs

The inputs to the development of a User Interface Prototype are:

- Prototyping plan that includes the scope of the user interface;
- Initial GUI Design;
- Application Style Guide;
- Task Scenarios;
- Users' Conceptual Models;
- Function Definitions;
- Usability Requirements.

4.9.4 Product: User Interface Prototype

What it is

A User Interface Prototype is a preliminary version or imitation of some or all of the user interface for the required system.

There are a number of different types:

- *Horizontal prototypes* provide full system access, but allow for only partial functionality;

- *Vertical prototypes* provide full functionality for a specified subset of the system;

- *Scenario-based prototypes* are a combination of the two types of prototypes outlined above. Such prototypes support interaction for a pre-defined set of tasks (usually a subset of the required tasks for the whole system).

User Interface Prototypes often lack qualities such as reliability and maintainability, in recognition of their limited life expectancy and utility. User Interface Prototypes may be thrown away once they have been tested *(throw-away prototypes)* or they may be evolved into the final system *(evolutionary prototypes)*. Throw-away prototypes are usually developed using a tool that allows them to be developed quickly, even if that tool cannot be used for the final system.

The product of User Interface Prototyping is a demonstrable and interactive example of the required user interface, albeit limited in some respects.

Where product is used

User Interface Prototyping is used:

- to refine the design of the GUI (Section 4.8);

- as the basis for evaluating the GUI (Section 4.10).

Quality Criteria

The quality criteria for User Interface Prototyping are:

1. Does the prototype address the objectives set out in the prototyping plan?

2. Does the prototype enable the assessment of Usability Requirements?

3. Is the prototype sufficiently realistic to allow the usability of the final system to be predicted?

4. Is the prototype exploring a technically feasible solution?

4.9.5 Effort and Skills

HCI skills are required to identify and recommend changes to the user interface design. Software engineering skills are required to develop, and subsequently modify, the User Interface Prototype to the required standard. Both of these skills are required to ensure the practicality of the prototype with respect to the development of the actual system.

The effort required to produce User Interface Prototypes must be commensurate with the objectives of the prototyping exercise. User Interface Prototyping may not be concerned with qualities such as maintainability and reliability. Therefore, good software engineering practices could be forsaken in favour of making resources available for iteratively modifying the prototype.

User Interface Prototyping can be split into a number of iterative cycles. The number of cycles required will depend upon the complexity of the interface, its importance, and the time it takes to reach agreement on the solution. Each prototyping cycle may be carried out in a 4 to 8 week time box, where:

> 2 to 4 weeks are spent on the design and development of the prototype;
>
> 1 to 2 weeks evaluating or demonstrating to users;
>
> 1 to 2 weeks identifying the changes, assessing their impact, and prioritising them.

4.9.6 Risks

User Interface Prototyping has many associated risks:

- users may gain an unrealistic impression of how

far a project has progressed;

- the data access component of the prototype is allowed to be developed into the final system rather than being thrown away;

- if not controlled using a technique such as impact analysis, then iterative prototyping can become an uncontrolled activity with no agreed end-point;

- the wrong tool may be used, giving a false impression of the intended solution;

- the user may form an unrealistic impression of the facilities to be provided in the final system;

- prototype development may require an uneconomic expenditure of valuable resources.

The possible risks have been more fully explored in the CCTA publication *Prototyping within an SSADM Environment* (1993)

4.9.7 References

Alavi (1984)
Browne (1994)
Budde, Kuhlenkamp, Mathiassen, and Zullighoven (1984)
CCTA (1993)

4.10 GUI Evaluation

4.10.1 Why do it?

GUI Evaluation is a technique for the assessment of the usability and suitability of a user interface design, as exemplified by a User Interface Prototype. GUI Evaluation produces deliverables which are used either to make modifications to the prototype, or as input to the GUI Design. The latter will allow inadequacies in the GUI Design, as exemplified by the prototype, to be addressed in subsequent steps.

There are two main reasons for GUI Evaluation:

- to determine the appropriateness of the proposed

Chapter 4
Techniques and Products

design of a user interface with respect to Usability Requirements;

- to provide a basis on which to make user interface improvements.

Without GUI Evaluation, a system might reach its intended users without its user interface being tested; it would represent the intentions of the systems designers, but these might not correspond to end-user requirements.

4.10.2 Description of Technique

GUI Evaluations are performed in the context of the documented Usability Requirements.

User evaluation should be carried out in co-operation with users, with the aim of eliciting useful feedback. This feedback must be documented in a form that allows it to direct the re-design or modification of the prototype.

Users are involved in interactive usability evaluation to note problems and opportunities for improvements. An impact analysis is performed to assess the benefits of proposed changes and the resources required to make those changes. In this way, the changes can be prioritised and iterative prototyping can be managed.

There are a number of specific techniques suitable for evaluating user interfaces. These fall into two main categories:

- Design Evaluation: evaluations that do not involve real users can be used to assess, among other things, whether the design supports all the user requirements and complies with the Application Style Guide. Such evaluations can be performed on design specifications, or by applying design audits and asking questions of best practice.

- Usability Evaluation: the usability of a design cannot be guaranteed without having representative samples of end-users actually interacting with a prototype or system. Such staged evaluations call upon a number of techniques, that will include:

73

- direct observation;
- video recording;
- software logging;
- interactive observation;
- 'thinking aloud' techniques.

The GUI Evaluation should be conducted as early as possible in the development process. Performing formative evaluations of paper-based prototypes or design specifications, before a computer based version is available, can be cost effective. However, paper-based prototypes cannot substitute for evaluations of interactive prototypes.

4.10.3 Inputs   The inputs to GUI Evaluation include:

- Usability Requirements, including usability criteria
- GUI Design
- User Interface Prototype
- Application Style Guide
- Function Definitions
- user support documentation
- end-users.

4.10.4 Product: Evaluation Report

What it is   The purpose of GUI Evaluation is to identify and document required changes to the user interface design. To meet this purpose, evaluations should deliver the following:

- an assessment of the extent to which Usability Requirements are satisfied;

- a list of problems as identified during the evaluations, and the impact of these problems in terms of business benefits;

- a list of proposed changes to address the identified problems, accompanied by an estimate of the resources required to make those changes;

- the impact of the problems and the cost of the

Chapter 4
Techniques and Products

changes consolidated within a prioritised list of changes; this impact analysis can then be used to control and manage the iterative prototyping activity;

- a set of changes to be made to the Application Style Guide.

Where product is used

The Evaluation Report is used:

- in GUI Design to identify areas for redesign (Section 4.8).

Quality Criteria

The quality criteria for GUI Evaluation are:

1. Have interactive evaluations been conducted under realistic conditions, considering the quality of the prototype, the representativeness of the users involved in the evaluation, the Task Scenarios supported by the prototype, and the realism of the data presented.

2. Has the feedback from the evaluation provided a basis for making design improvements?

3. Have the Usability Requirements been used to control and manage the evaluations?

4. Does the report assess whether the User Requirements are satisfied?

4.10.5 Effort and Skills

HCI analysis and design skills are required throughout the evaluation process. HCI expertise is required to plan, manage, and ensure the validity and reliability of all evaluations.

The effort required for evaluation will depend on the complexity of the system, the different user categories, and the number of end-users that will be involved with the GUI Evaluation.

GUI Evaluation should not be allowed to grow too large; small and frequent evaluations are more beneficial than one large evaluation at the end of the process.

SSADM and GUI Design: a Project Manager's Guide

Software engineers, familiar with the GUI environment, need to be involved in order to ratify the practicality and costs associated with design changes.

4.10.6 Risks

The value of GUI Evaluations can be undermined in a number of ways:

- the results of the evaluation are not fed back into the design-prototype-evaluate cycle.

- the purpose of evaluation on a project must not be forgotten: it is to deliver a usable system that will generate business benefits, as opposed to an exercise in testing interesting design alternatives;

- GUI Evaluations can become academic undertakings; the resources allotted to evaluation must be commensurate with the objectives of prototyping;

- GUI Evaluations are sometimes performed under unrealistic conditions that generate misleading findings.

4.10.7 References

Browne (1994)
Gilb (1984)
Good, Spine, Whiteside, and George (1986)
Hix and Hartson (1993)

5 Tailoring of the Default SSADM Structural Model

5.1 Introduction

This Chapter contains the required tailoring of the SSADM Version 4 Structural Model. Changes are identified in Stage diagrams as follows:

- amended and additional products are shown in *bold italic* ;

- additional steps are shown in bold boxes with *bold italic* step numbers and step names and the suffix 'GUI';

- amended SSADM steps are in bold boxes containing plain text step numbers and names and the suffix 'GUI';

- additional product flows are shown in bold arrows.

Two SSADM steps have been deleted: Step 350 (Develop Specification Prototypes); and Step 510 (Define User Dialogues). Step 350 has been deleted, since the prototyping of the GUI design at Step 365 will highlight any deficiencies in the Requirements Specification in the same way that Step 350 does in core SSADM V4. The difference is that the prototyping in Step 365 validates usability, and is typically incremental rather than throw-away; in other words, it moves towards a design product. Step 510 is deleted because its activities have been subsumed into the GUI design work in Stage 3.

There has been some debate over the placement of Step 365 within Stage 3, because the Step results in the production of a physical user interface design and, in most cases, the user interface which will be delivered as part of the final system. It is important to differentiate between the user interface component of the prototype and the data access component. Stages 4 to 6 of SSADM are still required to design the data access component of the target system, since this part of the user interface prototype should not normally be retained.

SSADM and GUI Design: a Project Manager's Guide

Another option would be to treat Step 365 as an SSADM Stage in its own right. For projects being managed under PRINCE, it is advisable to treat Step 365 as a PRINCE Stage, in order to limit the size of SSADM Stage 3, and allow the Project Board better control of the prototyping process. This alternative should be borne in mind during project planning.

The SSADM Version 4 Structural Model does not show iteration between steps that in practice always arises. In keeping with this, the tailored Structural Model in this chapter does not demonstrate the essentially iterative nature of development for a GUI design.

5.2 Stage 1

Overview

To understand the needs of the end users, it is essential to understand first the users' desires and capabilities. With this in mind, the amendments to Stage 1 ensure the users are analysed in more depth than currently required by core SSADM. The detailed descriptions of the users are documented in the extended User Catalogue. By early identification and documentation of the classes of users who will interact with the system, the analysts will be able to focus system development on the specific requirements of the real user population rather than their representatives (e.g. supervisors and user line management).

Alongside the user analysis runs the development of models of the users' tasks. During task modelling it will be possible to identify those tasks which users find difficult, and which should therefore be supported by technology (if possible); and those tasks which they enjoy and which therefore should be left in the users' hands to avoid demotivation. Other factors which drive the allocation of tasks to the users or the computer system include job design, performance, cost errors, and training.

Due to a considerable overlap of information with the Task Models, the Current System Data Flow Model will

Chapter 5
Tailoring of the Default SSADM Structural Model

be simplified at the lower levels. It could be decided to produce only a high-level Data Flow Model, with Task Models providing the detailed descriptions of the user-based processing. An important point to raise here is that, while the Current System Data Flow Model may be considered optional, Task Models should always be produced.

In core SSADM, the users' view of the processing is overridden when the Logical Data Flow Model is produced. In order to maintain the focus on the users rather than on the system needs, the Task Models must be retained in parallel with the Logical Data Flow Model. Logical Data Flow Diagrams will be produced to a sufficient level of detail to support I/O Descriptions without duplicating detailed information on the Task Models.

The method of development of the Current System Logical Data Model is unchanged, but information to be recorded in the Logical Data Model can be derived from the Task Models.

Just as 'standard' functional and non-functional requirements are initially documented during Stage 1 and expanded during subsequent stages, the Usability Requirements need to be elicited and made explicit. These will be the foundation for design and assessment of the user interface in later stages. The basis of Usability Requirements will as usual be the business objectives factored down to the system objectives. The system objectives will provide the analyst with the ability to quantify and prioritise the Usability Requirements.

Inputs (additional)	None
Inputs (amended)	None
Inputs (deleted)	None
Products (additional)	Current Task Models
Products (amended)	Extended User Catalogue (replaces User Catalogue)

SSADM and GUI Design: a Project Manager's Guide

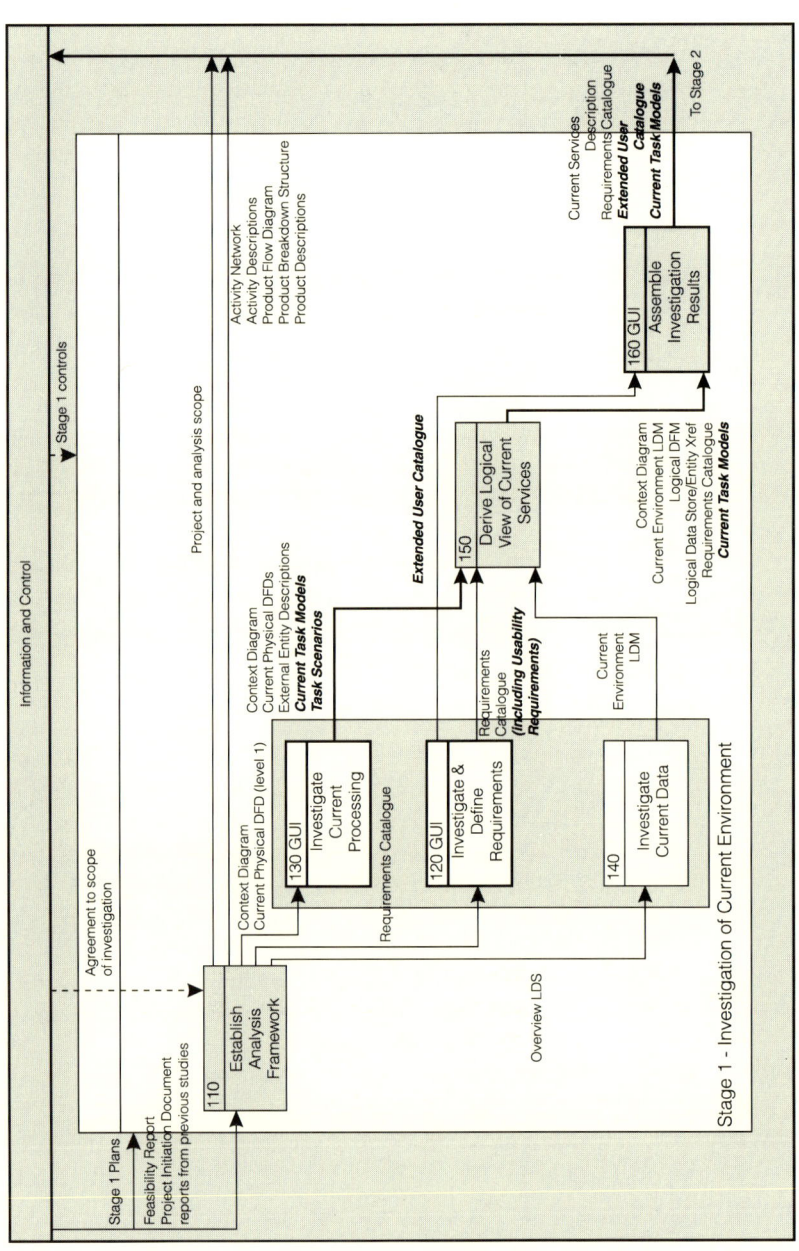

Figure 5-1: SSADM Structural Model - Stage 1

Products (deleted)	None
Techniques (additional)	User Analysis (performed in Step 120 Task 20) Task Analysis (performed in Step 130 as part of Task Modelling)

5.3 Stage 2

Overview

The Current Task Models and the user characteristics are used when deciding on possible system boundaries. The Current Task Models provide an excellent means of obtaining the user view of the processing that should be included in the Business System Options (BSOs). The Extended User Catalogue will guide the analysts in deciding the feasibility of BSOs from the end users' point of view.

The possible and selected system boundaries are shown on the high-level logical Data Flow Diagram and on the Current Task Models.

It is important to note that, as selecting the BSO defines the user tasks in the Required System, some elementary prototyping of the user interface is probably desirable during this stage. This necessitates the selection of the GUI standard (eg Motif or Windows) in Stage 2 rather than in Stage 4. Even if prototyping does not take place in Stage 2, the GUI standard needs to be selected before GUI design takes place in the new Step 365.

Inputs (additional)	Installation Style Guide Current Task Models
Inputs (amended)	Extended User Catalogue
Inputs (deleted)	None
Products (additional)	None
Products (amended)	None
Products (deleted)	None

Techniques (additional)   User Task Allocation
User Interface Prototyping

5.4   Stage 3

Overview   Following the selection of the Business System Option, the users' Current Task Models are suitably modified to match the new, amended, or deleted tasks to be performed with the new system.

The new Task Models will identify the information needs of the users, as well as providing an outline view of their processing needs. Using the Required System Task Models and the BSO, the Required System Data Flow Model and Logical Data Model are developed alongside the Users' Conceptual Models. Users do not separate data from processing, and they have a picture of what the system is doing to provide them with their information needs. Users' Conceptual Models allow developers to record the users' holistic view of the system they are using. There is obvious synergy between the Users' Conceptual Models and the system data and processing requirements; so these activities are performed in parallel, but probably by different development staff.

Note that it may be decided that there is no need to produce a Required System Data Flow Model: this decision will depend largely on the focus of development activities. For instance, a new system with complex system processing may well benefit from the production of a Data Flow Model; whereas the production of a GUI front-end to 'legacy systems' will benefit little from such work. Whatever the situation, since DFDs are working documents, it may be decided to proceed straight from logical DFDs to Function Definition.

After the parallel development of the system processing, and the data and user views of the required system, Functions can be more easily defined to meet the users' requirements. There is no need to produce I/O

Chapter 5
Tailoring of the Default SSADM Structural Model

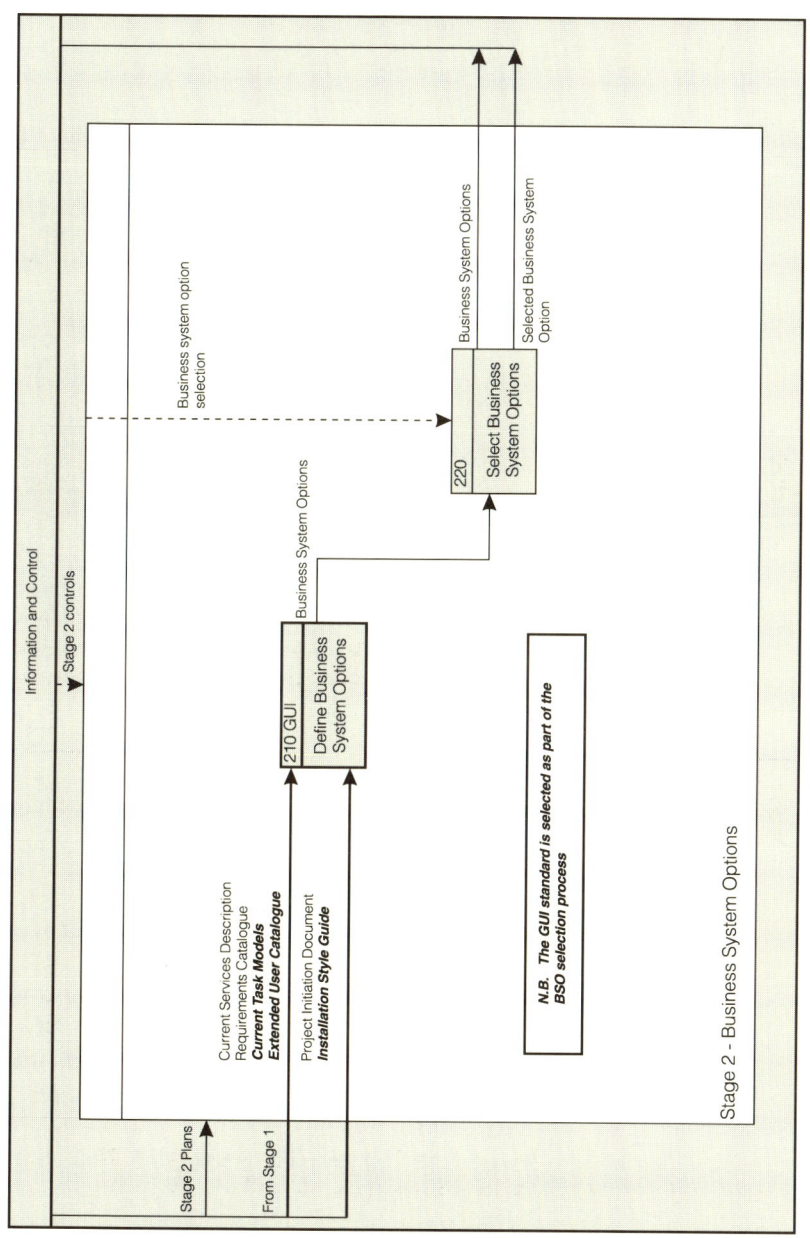

Figure 5-2: SSADM Structural Model - Stage 2

Structures during Function Definition. However, it is necessary to record the grouping, selection, and iteration of user I/O. These can be represented either by fragmented I/O Structures or by annotated I/O Descriptions. The aim is to record the necessary system responses to user data without imposing a particular order of working. These modified I/O Structures will ultimately be replaced as a result of the production of the GUI Design.

Function Definitions contain the same information as in core SSADM; however, the inputs to their production are supplemented. The Users' Conceptual Model provides a view of how the users bundle system objects and their associated actions together. The Required Task Models provide information on the way that users wish to bundle processing together.

In parallel with Function Definition, the Application Style Guide is produced based on the Installation Style Guide, referring to the Task Models to ensure that a suitable set of information containers are provided.

The remaining steps of SSADM Stage 3 continue unchanged through Relational Data Analysis, Entity Event Modelling, and Enquiry Access Paths, since these are all concerned with the internal logical data manipulation.

In the new Step 365, a complete GUI Design is produced. The design will include all aspects of the user interface, including outline help facilities and error messages which are normally left until Stages 5 and 6. The reason for this is that the help is provided at the user interface to handle errors and areas of possible confusion are just as important as the support to normal working. However, detailed help text can be developed later in Stage 6.

The inclusion of a 'design' activity within Stage 3 appears at first sight to be in conflict with the separation of the logical and physical aspects of the system, which is a fundamental concept in SSADM. However, both the iterative nature of GUI Design, and the participation of users will cause many new requirements to be

Chapter 5
Tailoring of the Default SSADM Structural Model

discovered which will impact the Stage 3 products. For this reason, it was decided to include GUI Design in Stage 3 rather than within Stage 5 or as a separate stage. It must be emphasised that the GUI Design only describes the user interface. It does not include the internal system design, which takes place in Stage 6.

There are obvious benefits in developing the GUI Design on the technology targetted for the final system. The constraint this imposes is that the GUI environment must be known. It does not imply that other aspects of the target platform, such as the DBMS, are known, as many GUI development environments are independent of such considerations. The completed GUI Design may be completely automated, or may be completely paper-based. However, it is most likely that it will be a combination of the two, with critical interactions being prototyped using automation.

During GUI Design, the Users' Conceptual Models aid the analysts in deciding which information should be presented graphically; how the overall system should be presented, together with navigation through the components of the GUI; and how to position textual information to meet the user view of how the data is organised. The Task Scenarios are used to test paths through the GUI Design.

As the prototyping and evaluation activities refine the GUI Design, the Required System Task Models may well be amended. In effect, the Required System Task Models provide the basis for the development of the User Manual, in that they provide detailed descriptions of the activities and information needs of users when interacting with the system.

The production of GUI prototypes and final design may necessitate the development of some skeleton data base functionality. This should be treated purely as prototype material. It should have no impact on Enquiry Access Paths, Effect Correspondence Diagrams, nor Process Models. It should be discarded after Stage 3, though useful information (such as response requirements elicited) should be recorded for later database and

SSADM and GUI Design: a Project Manager's Guide

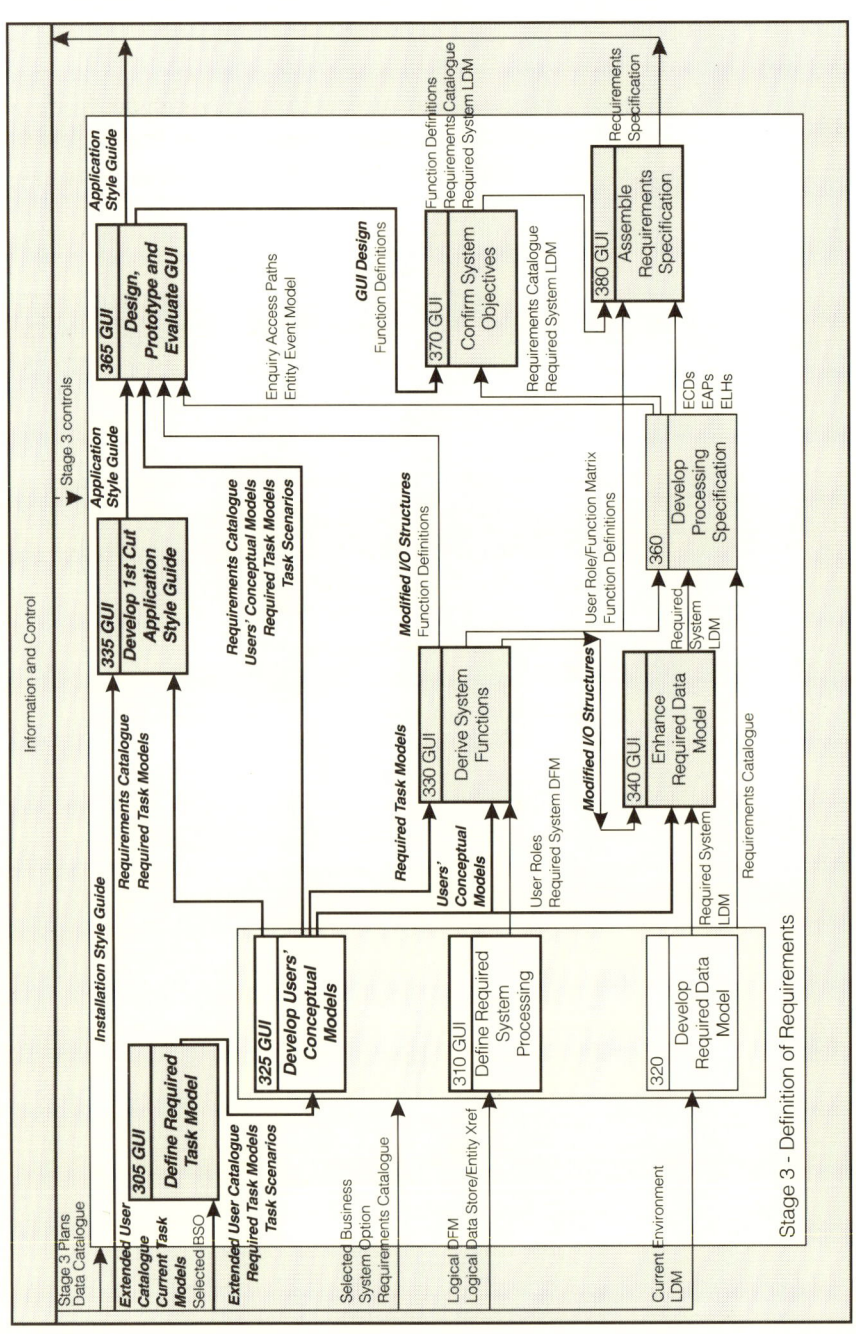

Figure 5-3: SSADM Structural Model - Stage 3

Chapter 5
Tailoring of the Default SSADM Structural Model

processing design.

Step 350 Develop Specification Prototypes has been removed from Stage 3, since the verification of functional requirements will occur during the broader activities in the new Step 365. Indeed, specification prototyping needs to be stronger for GUI Design, and must be carried out more effectively. This can be achieved in the context of prototyping and evaluating the interface as the users will eventually see it. The evaluation of the interface, with real end-users wherever possible, ensures that all the required functionality is identified.

Inputs (additional)	None
Inputs (amended)	Extended User Catalogue Current Task Models Installation Style Guide
Inputs (deleted)	Prototyping Scope
Inputs (deleted)	None
Products (additional)	None
Products (amended)	Application Style Guide
Products (deleted)	Command Structures Menu Structures Prototyping Report
Techniques (additional)	Task Modelling Task Scenario Definition Style Guide Definition User Conceptual Modelling GUI Design User Interface Prototyping GUI Evaluation

5.5 Stage 4

Overview

The GUI standard and the prototype development environment are selected in Stage 2. This does not constrain the more detailed selection of the target platform. The emphasis in Stage 4 will be on activities such as meeting the performance and sizing requirements, and designing the distribution of data and processing.

The development of the Application Style Guide is no longer a part of Stage 4, since it has been developed during Stage 3.

Inputs (additional)	None
Inputs (amended)	Application Style Guide
Inputs (deleted)	None
Products (additional)	None
Products (amended)	Application Style Guide
Products (deleted)	None
Techniques (additional)	None

Chapter 5
Tailoring of the Default SSADM Structural Model

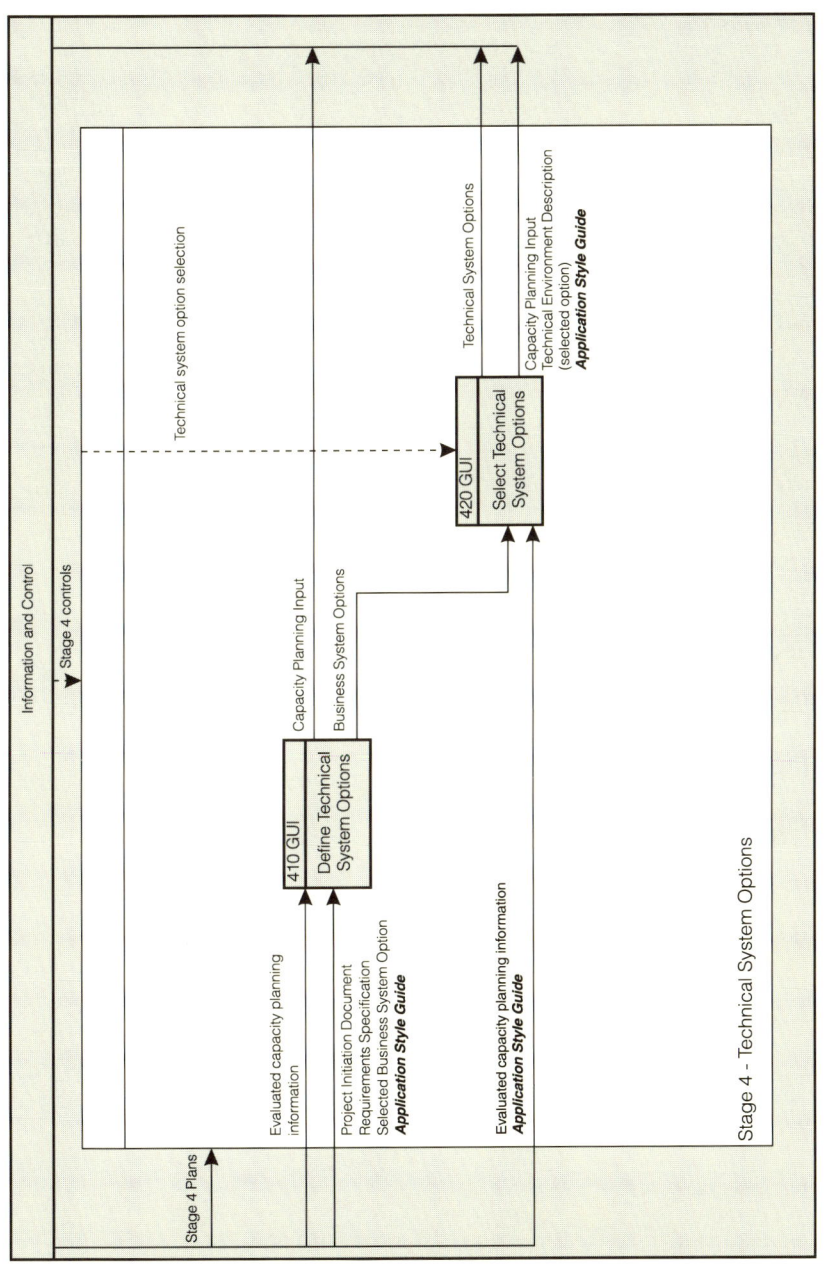

Figure 5-4: SSADM Structural Model - Stage 4

SSADM and GUI Design: a Project Manager's Guide

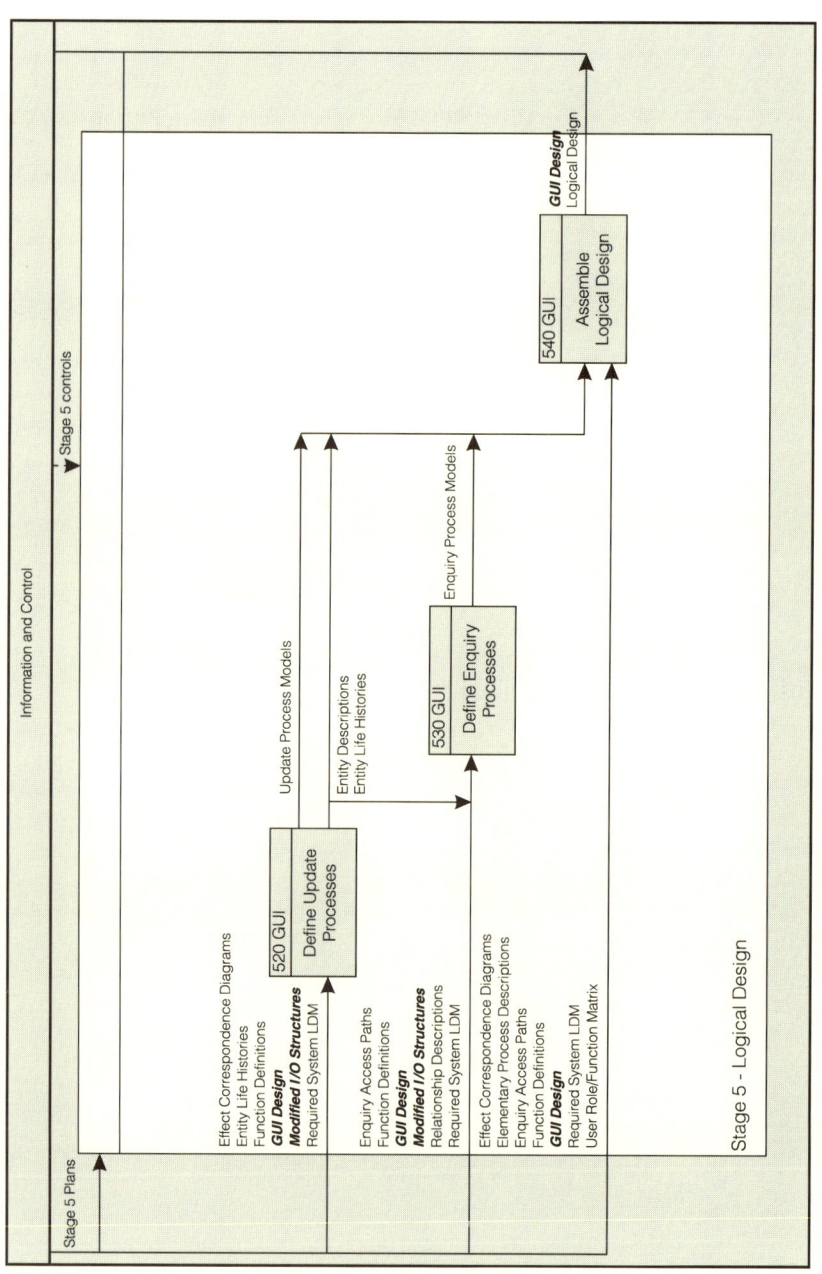

Figure 5-5: SSADM Structural Model - Stage 5

Chapter 5
Tailoring of the Default SSADM Structural Model

5.6 Stage 5

Overview

Since all the user interface design has been completed in Stage 3, Step 510 Define User Dialogues is redundant, and has been deleted from Stage 5. This means that the SSADM dialogue-related products are no longer required in the Logical Design. In other words, the following products are no longer delivered: Command Structures, Dialogue Control Tables, Dialogue Level Help, Dialogue Structures, and Menu Structures. All these products are targetted at traditional menu-based interfaces, and are not relevant to a GUI.

Since I/O Structures are no longer produced in the way defined in core SSADM, developers should choose what they are going to use as the input to Logical Database Process Design. The modified I/O Structures are nearest to what developers know; however, the GUI Design represents in more detail the flow of I/O at the user interface.

Inputs (additional)   GUI Design

Inputs (amended)   Modified I/O Structures

Inputs (deleted)   None

Products (additional)   GUI Design

Products (amended)   None

Products (deleted)   Command Structures
                               Dialogue Control Tables
                               Dialogue Level Help
                               Dialogue Structures
                               Menu Structures

Techniques (additional)   None

5.7 Stage 6

Overview

During Step 630, GUI elements are linked to the appropriate processing specifications within the Function Component Implementation Map.

In Step 650, GUI Design may be refined to meet the requirements of performance, a specific platform, and any new tool capabilities being exploited, following selection of the target environment in Stage 4.

The GUI Design is updated to include details of error processing which it has not been possible to include without knowledge of the Physical Design.

Inputs (additional)	GUI Design
Inputs (amended)	Application Style Guide
Inputs (deleted)	None
Products (additional)	None
Products (amended)	GUI Design
Products (deleted)	None
Techniques (additional)	None

Chapter 5
Tailoring of the Default SSADM Structural Model

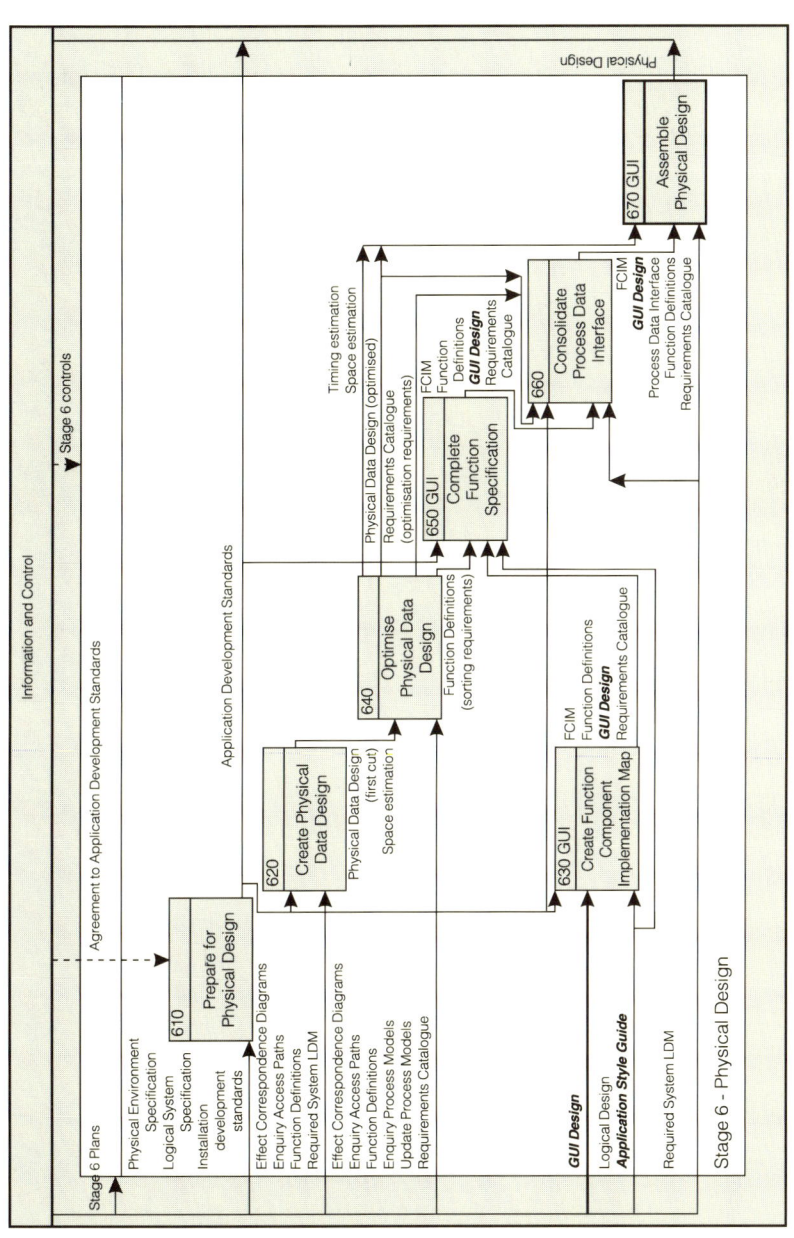

Figure 5-6: SSADM Structural Model - Stage 6

6 Tailored approaches to systems development using SSADM Version 4

6.1 Introduction

The SSADM Reference Manual describes a default approach containing all the analysis and design activities and products which may be relevent to the development of a large information system. It is a generic approach, capable of being used in a wide variety of project circumstances. SSADM should be tailored to meet the specific requirements of individual projects.

SSADM Version 4 has been designed to allow maximum flexibility. This preliminary guide has described extensions to the method which maximise its benefits in a GUI environment. There are, however, many other ways in which SSADM can be adapted for various situations and development environments.

In order to ensure that all such guidance is consistent and compatible with SSADM's underlying principles, a system development template has been introduced as part of the SSADM rationale. This template breaks system development into a number of distinct areas of concern. For the purposes of this guide, these major areas are:

- Investigation
- Specification
- User Environment
- Decision Structure
- Policies and Procedures
- Construction.

These areas of concern are shown in the system development template in Figure 6-1.

The 'specification' component of this template is further sub-divided to contain three important classifications of system products:

- Conceptual Model
- External Design
- Internal Design.

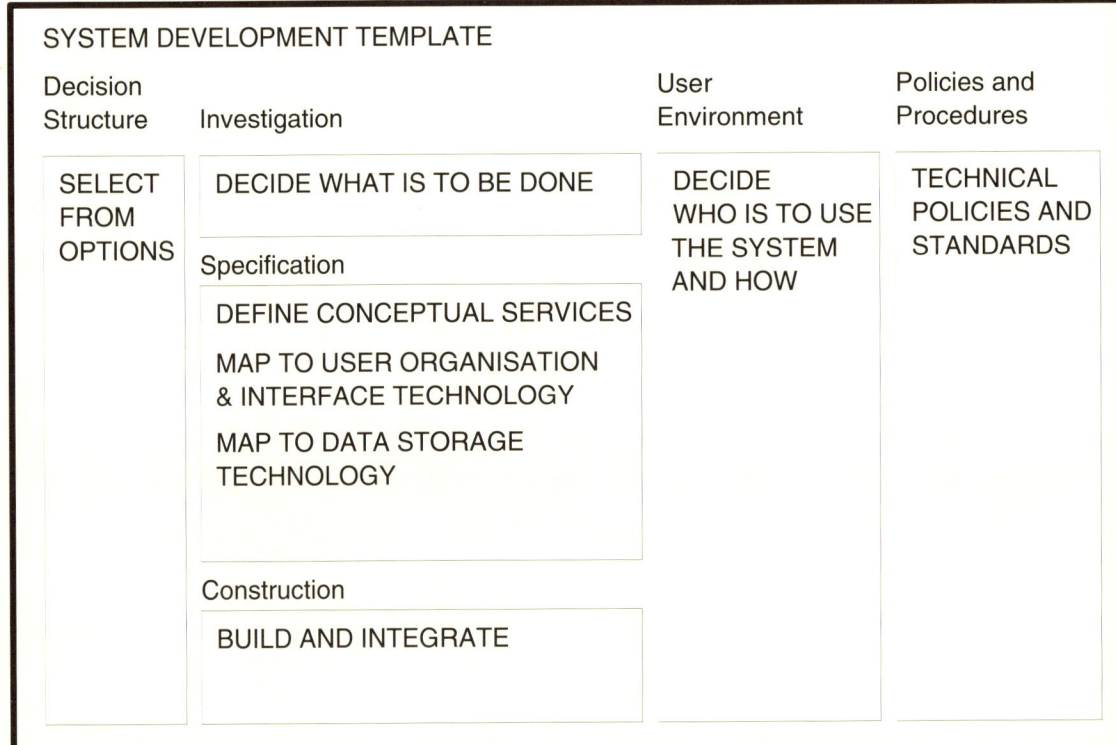

Figure 6-1: System Development Template

These three parts are collectively known as the 3-schema specification architecture, and are described in outline within this chapter.

Tailored versions of SSADM should be mapped onto the system development template, with particular attention being paid to the 3-Schema specification architecture.

6.2   The system development template and the 3-schema specification architecture

Figure 6-2 provides an example of the use of the system development template by the mapping of the products of core SSADM as defined in the Version 4 Reference Manual.

Chapter 6
Tailored approaches to systems development using SSADM Version 4

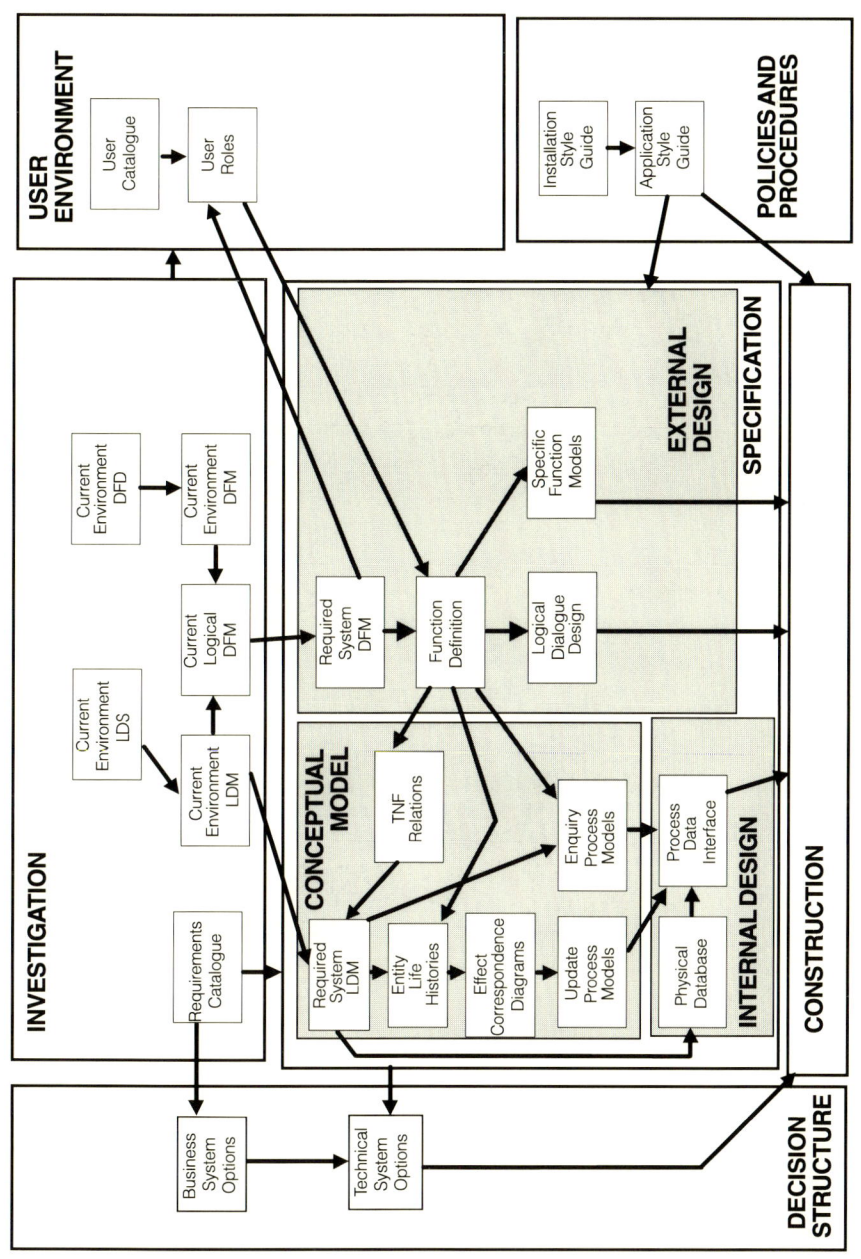

Figure 6-2 : System development template and 3-schema architecture

The 3-schema specification architecture can be used to divide system specification into three parallel development strands. These extend the separation of concerns already demonstrated within the SSADM Version 4 Reference Manual via the Universal Function Model.

The Conceptual Model defines the essential business rules and knowledge, expressed in a Logical Data Model and Entity-Event Models. This is a system model which is independent of the user interface, and portable between implementation environments. It can be implemented as logical database processes which apparently read and write entities in the Logical Data Model. For the design of the Conceptual Model, it is possible to believe that there is in some sense a 'right answer'. Through the use of stereotype components and a disciplined approach to Entity-Event Modelling, the designer can produce a highly objective procedural specification of the database processing. All elements of the Conceptual Model will ultimately be implemented in the resulting computer system.

The External Design defines the user interface including data definitions for input/output files, screens, and reports; and process definitions for dialogue and batch input/output programs. There are two levels of consideration within External Design. The mapping of business services onto User Roles and the mapping of these Roles onto interface technology. The External Design depends on trade-offs between a number of different things such as organisation structure; ergonomics; system efficiency; input-output device technology; arbitary preferences of particular users; audit principles; security; user politics, etc.

The Internal Design defines the physical data design (perhaps tuned for performance reasons) and the Process/Data Interface including elementary data storage and retrieval processes. These deal with reading and writing individual records from the physical database, so that conceptual processes can act as though they read and write entities in the Logical Data Model. The Internal Design also depends on trade-offs between a

Chapter 6
Tailored approaches to systems development using SSADM Version 4

number of things whose relative importance is subjectively defined such as: time objectives; space objectives; maintainability. Once again, this implies that there is no one 'right answer', and that a heuristic, prototyping approach may be needed.

The 3-schema specification architecture concentrates on those products that will ultimately turn into code. The system development template takes a broader view, and enables us to identify products which feed into and are developed from those described within the 3-schema specification architecture. This particular guide is able to make significant use of the 'User Environment' component of the system development template and shows how the products allocated to this part of the template interface to those within the 3-schema specification architecture.

6.3 User-centered design and the system development template

Figure 6-3 is an example of the GUI product flow diagram within this guide mapped onto the System Development Template, with particular emphasis on the interface to the specification component described via the 3-schema specification architecture.

This diagram shows that SSADM/GUI involves change in just three areas: Investigation; User Environment; and External Design. There is no change whatsoever to the SSADM Conceptual Model, Internal Design, Construction, Decision Structure, or Policies and Procedures. Investigation is only changed in a small way: the Requirements Catalogue is extended to emphasise Usability Requirements; and a Current Task Model is developed.

There are, however, important additions to the User Environment area, where three new products are introduced:

- User Class Descriptions;
- Required Task Models;
- Task Scenarios.

SSADM and GUI Design: a Project Manager's Guide

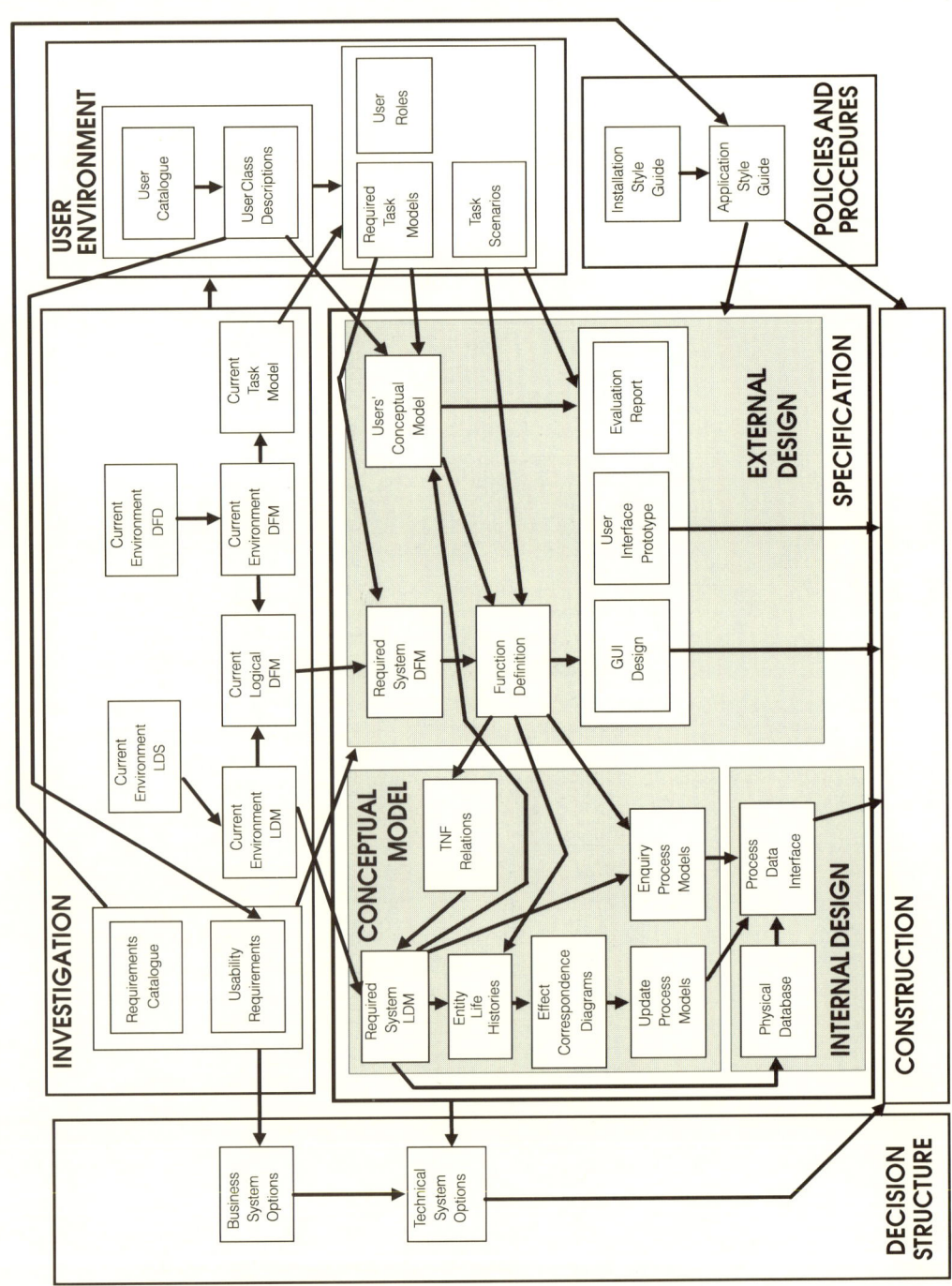

Figure 6-3: Mapping of Product Flow Diagram onto system development template

These provide a more detailed picture than core SSADM of who the users are, what they are trying to achieve, and how they perform their tasks. This is essential for a user-centered approach to application development.

External Design has four new products:

- Users' Conceptual Model;
- GUI Design;
- User Interface Prototype;
- Evaluation Report.

In addition to these new products, there is a change from core SSADM in the way the External Design is created, evolved, and validated. Usually, the system internals are designed first (entities, events, functions, etc) and the detailed user interface added later. What the end-user will actually see is not known until Stages 5 or 6. Unless Specification Prototyping is used for this purpose, there is no activity performed specifically to confirm the usability of the user interface.

By contrast, this SSADM/GUI guide recommends:

- modelling users and their tasks, environment, and usability requirements earlier in the development;

- developing an abstract definition of how the user thinks of the system (Users' Conceptual Model). This must be comprehensible to the users and useful for their tasks, and be capable of being mapped onto the SSADM Conceptual Model (Logical Data Model, Entity-Event Models, etc).

- developing this abstract view into the more concrete External Design products of Function Definitions and GUI Design;

- prototyping and evaluating the initial GUI Design with real end-users, and iteratively redesigning it until the GUI Design satisfies usability requirements.

It is this user-centered design approach, with its

emphasis on end-users and usability, that complements core SSADM and leads to the additional products shown in Figure 6-3.

Bibliography

Alavi M (1984) *An assessment of the prototyping approach to information systems development* Communications of the ACM 27(6) pp 556-563

Apple Computer Inc (1992) *Macintosh Human Interface Guidelines.* Addison-Wesley ISBN 0 201 62216 5

Baecker R M and Buxton W A S (1987) *Readings in Human-Computer Interaction: A Multi-Disciplinary Approach.* Morgan Kaufman, Los Altos, California ISBN 0 934613 24 9

Browne D P (1994) *STUDIO : STructured User-interface Design for Interaction Optimisation.* Prentice Hall ISBN 0 13 014721 4

Budde R, Kuhlenkamp K, Mathiassen L, and Zullighoven H (1984) *Approaches to prototyping.* Springer-Verlag

Card S, Moran T and Newell A (1983) *The Psychology of Human-Computer Interaction.* Lawrence Erlbaum Associates.

CCTA (1991a) *User Interface: Style Guide Issues*

CCTA (1991b) *User Interface: Style Migration Issues*

CCTA (1993) *Prototyping within an SSADM Environment*

Cox K and Walker D (1993) *User Interface Design.* Prentice Hall ISBN 0 13 95288 1

Diaper D (1989) *Task Analysis for Human-Computer Interaction.* Ellis Horwood ISBN 13 884487 9

Gilb T (1984) *The impact analysis table applied to human factors design*, Proceedings of Interact 84, First IFIP Conference on Human-Computer Interaction, Amsterdam, September 4-7, Vol. 2, pp 97-101. Elsevier

Good M, Spine T M, Whiteside J, and George P (1986)

User-derived impact analysis as a tool for usability engineering CHI86 Proceedings, pp 241-6.

Gould J D, Boies S J, Levy S, Richards J T and Scoonard J (1990) *The 1984 Olympic Message System: A Test of Behavioural Principles of System Design* in Preece J and Keller L (eds) *Human-Computer Interaction.* Prentice Hall ISBN 0 13 444910 X

Helander M (ed) (1988) *Handbook of Human-Computer Interaction* Elsevier ISBN 0 444 70536 8

Hix D and Hartson H R (1993) *Developing User Interfaces: Ensuring Usability through Product and Process.* Wiley ISBN XXX0 471 53846 9.

Horton W (1991) *Illustrating Computer Documentation.* Wiley. ISBN 0 471 53846 9.

HUFIT (1990) *HUFIT Planning, Analysis and Specification Toolset.* HUSAT Research Institute, University of Loughborough (User Mapping and User Characteristics tools).

IBM (1991) Systems Application Architecture Common User Access (SAA CUA). A series of documents is available from IBM Technical Publication Centres describing the details of Common User Access:

> SAA CUA Guide to User Interface Design (document number SC34-4289-00). Describes the process of interface design for CUA91 and the workplace.

> SAA CUA Guide to Advanced Interface Design Reference (document number SC34-4290-00). Provides an alphabetic reference guide to each of the interface components in CUA91

ISO TC159/SC4/WG5 (1990) *Usability Assurance Statements* ISO CD 9241-11 version 2.5.

Laurel B (ed) (1990) *The Art of Human-Computer Interface Design.* Addison-Wesley ISBN 0 201 51797 3

Bibliography

Marcus A (1992) *Graphic Design for Electronic Documents and User Interfaces*. ACM Press Tutorial Series ISBN 0 201 54364 8

Mayhew D J (1992) *Principles and Guidelines in Software User Interface Design*. Prentice Hall ISBN 0 13 721929 6

Microsoft (1992) *The Windows Interface, an Application Design Guide*. Microsoft Press ISBN 1 55615 384 8

Nielsen J (ed) (1989) *Coordinating User Interfaces for Consistency*. Academic Press ISBN 0 12 518400 X.

Norman D A (1988) *The Psychology of Everyday Things*, Basic Books, New York ISBN 0 465 06709 3

Norman D A and Draper S W (eds) (1986) *User Centered System Design. New Perspectives in Human Computer Interaction*. Lawrence Erlbaum Associates, Hillsdale, N.J. ISBN 0 89859 781 1

Open University (1990) *Course manuals for postgraduate course on Human-Computer Interaction*. PMT 607 Open University.

Open University (1990) *A Guide to Usability*. Published in association with the Department of Trade and Industry ISBN 0 7492 4344 9

OSF/MOTIF (1993) *OSF/Motif Style Guide, Revision 1.2*. Prentice-Hall ISBN 0 13 643123 2

Peters T J and Waterman R H (1982) *In Search of Excellence: Lessons from America's Best-Run Companies*. Harper and Row ISBN 0 06 015042 4

Robinson K and Berrisford G (1994) *Object-Oriented SSADM*. Prentice Hall ISBN 0 13 309444 8

Rouse W B (1991) *Design for Success: A Human-Centered Approach to Designing Successful Products and Systems*. Wiley Interscience.

Rubinstein R and Hersh H M (1984) *The Human Factor:*

Designing Computer Systems for People. Digital Press, Bedford, M.A. ISBN 0 932376 44 4

Scneiderman B (1992) *Designing the User Interface: Strategies for Effective Human-Computer Interaction*. (2nd edition) Addison-Wesley ISBN 0 201 57286 9

Thimbleby H (1990) *User Interface Design*. Addison Wesley ISBN 0 201 41618 2

Tognazzini B (1992) *Tog on Interface,* Addison-Wesley ISBN 0 201 60842 1

Tufte E.R. (1983) *The Visual Display of Quantitative Information*, Graphics Press.

Glossary of Terms

allocation of tasks	The process of apportionment of tasks between user roles and the system. This needs to be performed at a number of levels.
application style guide	A document that defines the appearance and behaviour of a user interface to one or more applications. See also *Installation Style Guide*.
character based	IT systems that interact with users through dumb terminals or terminal emulators.
conceptual view	The model users form in their minds of how a system is organised and operated.
current task models	Task descriptions which show the key parts of the way the current system is operated.
desktop	A graphical user interface that uses the office desktop as a metaphor. Typically, desktops will mimic common office objects and operations such as storing a document in a folder.
direct manipulation	Refers to a system where the user uses a mouse to perform actions on objects displayed on the screen, and the user is given constant feedback on the results of those actions.
end-users	The persons who have hands-on experience of a system. An end-user is an actual person using the system.
evaluation	The process of comparing the system and the user interface against some pre-defined goals, with the aim of identifying areas for improvement. See also *usability evaluation*.
evolutionary prototyping	The process of growing a system through prototyping.
extended user catalogue	A documented profile of users. This will probably include details of skills held and tasks performed by various user roles.

external event	Events which start tasks, such as a phone call, a request, or some information becoming available to the user.
first-cut user task analysis	The initial documented findings from an investigation of the activities performed by users. These findings remain to be validated.
GUI	Graphical User Interface, where each point on the screen (pixel) can be individually addressed. This allows the use of multiple character fonts and drawing capabilities. GUI devices usually support a WIMP interface.
HCI	Human-Computer Interaction. The interaction of users with Information Technology (IT) systems.
HCI experts	Individuals who are recognised by their peers as having skills in the discipline of Human Computer Interaction.
help system	Assistance on the performance of tasks provided to end-users. It is most often used to refer to on-line interactive help.
horizontal prototype	A prototype that only contains the main system functions and does not go into the detailed design of functionality. See also *vertical* and *scenario based prototypes*.
hypertext system	A system that supports multiple means of navigating through texts. Navigation in a hypertext system is typically supported by hot-buttons (mouse sensitive areas) in the text. Invoking a hot-button results in a related piece of text being displayed.
icon	Graphical representation of an object or concept.
installation style guide	A style guide to be applied across all of the applications within a corporation. Its purpose is to ensure the consistency of the 'look-and-feel' of multiple applications. Also known as an organisation style guide.
interface design	The specification for the interactive aspects of a system.
ISO 9241	A set of standards specific to Human-Computer Interaction produced by the International Standards Organisation.

Glossary of Terms

look-and-feel	Generalisations regarding the appearance and behaviour of a user interface.
mental model	Users' cognitive representation of some object(s) or process(es). That is the users' understanding of how something will look or behave, as opposed to how something will actually appear or operate.
metaphor	A representation used for purposes of explanation that is based on a commonly understood frame of reference. For instance, graphical user interfaces are frequently represented as an office desktop.
Microsoft Windows	A popular graphical user interface environment.
navigation standards	Rules that stipulate how users are to be supported with respect to accessing the functionality of a system.
object-oriented analysis	An analysis technique that focuses on objects as opposed to data, processes, or functions.
object-oriented methods	Methods developed for use on projects adopting the object-oriented paradigm.
OSF	Open Software Foundation. An organisation set up by a number of leading IT suppliers to develop an open systems environment. The user interface of this environment is OSF/Motif.
prototype	A working example of the system, or a subset of it, which allows users and developers to interact with it.
required task model	The definition of the task as it is intended that it will be performed with the new system.
scenario based prototype	A prototype that supports the completion of specific predefined tasks, contained in a scenario.
stakeholder	Someone who is associated with the results or input to the new system, but may not be an end-user.
task	Activities that users undertake in order to achieve some goal. A task has a definable start and end point.

task design	The organisation of work into tasks, and the relationships between those tasks.
task goal	The purpose of performing a task, the attainment of which marks the completion of the task.
task model	A model that depicts the actions to be undertaken in order to complete a specific task.
task scenario	An example of an actual task, such as answering the question "where does the Number 49 bus stop".
task scenario type	A task scenario type is a way of grouping scenarios to ensure that there are sufficient scenarios to ensure coverage. Scenarios dealing with queries about bus routes would all be of the same type.
top-level menu (top menu)	The highest level of structuring imposed on a user's interaction with a system. This structure is normally presented as a set of choices from which one selection can be made at a time.
usability	Defined by ISO as being "the degree to which specific users can achieve specific goals in a particular environment with effectiveness, efficiency and satisfaction".
usability criteria	Levels of usability that need to be met by a system.
usability defects	Aspects of a user interface design that fail to meet the usability criteria established for the system.
usability evaluations	Exercises undertaken to test whether a system or intended system is likely to meet the usability criteria established for it.
usability metrics	Measures of the usability of a user interface.
usability requirements	Needs that should be met by a system that relate to the usability of that system.
users	The persons who are or will be impacted by an IT system.

Glossary of Terms

user analysis	An examination of the roles, skills, and usage patterns of users.
user class	A collection of users who have important characteristics in common.
users' conceptual model	A model of the objects and relationships in the system, as understood by the user.
user class description	A report and a set of tables that describe the different users of the system.
user environment	The situation in which users of IT will find themselves. The user environment is considered as everything that impacts their interaction with the IT system. This may include such things as peripheral equipment, telephones, and documentation.
user group	A set of individuals who represent the end-users of the existing or proposed system.
user interface	The point of interaction between users and IT systems.
user interface consistency	The similarities in the presentation and operation of the various facets of a user interface.
user task allocation	The distribution of tasks between different users or user roles.
vertical prototype	A prototype that provides full functionality for a subset of user tasks.
window design	The layout, visual contents, and actions associated with a particular window.
windows	A major component of all Graphical User Interfaces. A Window is an area of screen space having definite boundaries and its own contents. While many windows may be open simultaneously, only one is active and responding to user interactions at any moment.
WIMP	An interface that incorporates Windows, Icons, Menus and Pointers.

Printed in the United Kingdom for HMSO
Dd296946 4/94 C8 G3397 10170